# It's So Christmas-See!

A Collection Of Resources For Thanksgiving And Christmas

**Janet Burton**
**Robert V. Dodd**
**Donna J. Fetzer**
**Adalya Hadar**
**Arthur J. L. Meether**
**Jeanne Mueller**
**Myra Shofner**
**Judy Gattis Smith**
**Bill Thomas**
**Louis H. Valbracht**
**Judith Hale Wood**

CSS Publishing Company, Inc., Lima, Ohio

IT'S SO CHRISTMAS-SEE!

Copyright © 2007 by
CSS Publishing Company, Inc.
Lima, Ohio

The original purchaser may photocopy material in this publication for use as it was intended (i.e., worship material for worship use; educational material for classroom use; dramatic material for staging or production). No additional permission is required from the publisher for such copying by the original purchaser only. Inquiries should be addressed to: Permissions, CSS Publishing Company, Inc., 517 South Main Street, Lima, Ohio 45804.

Most scripture quotations are from the New Revised Standard Version of the Bible, copyright 1989 by the Division of Christian Education of the National Council of the Churches of Christ in the USA. Used by permission.

Some scripture quotations are from the New American Standard Bible © 1960, 1962, 1963, 1968, 1971, 1973, 1975, 1977 by The Lockman Foundation. Used by permission.

*Come! See What God Has Done* by Jeanne Mueller and Judith Hale Wood was originally published by CSS Publishing Company in 1981. ISBN: 0-89536-508-1. It was revised and printed in *In Search Of Christmas* published by CSS Publishing Company in 2002.

*A Drama For Thanksgiving (In One Act)* by Arthur J. L. Meether was originally published by CSS Publishing Company in 1976. ISBN: 0-89536-057-8.

"Is It Still Wonderful?" was originally published in *High Days, Holy Days And HoliDaze* by Louis H. Valbracht, published by CSS Publishing Company in 1973. ISBN: 0-89536-093-4.

"Welcome The Spirit Of Christmas" was originally published in *Worship Innovations: Hanging The Greens* by Janet Burton, published by CSS Publishing Company in 2000. ISBN: 0-7880-1759-4.

*A Christmas Remembrance* by Arthur J. L. Meether was originally published by CSS Publishing Company in 1976. ISBN: 0-89536-045-4.

For more information about CSS Publishing Company resources, visit our website at www.csspub.com or email us at csr@csspub.com or call (800) 241-4056.

Cover design by Barbara Spencer
ISBN-13: 978-0-7880-2461-0
ISBN-10: 0-7880-2461-2

PRINTED IN USA

# Table Of Contents

**Come! See What God Has Done** — 5
    A Thanksgiving Event For Children
        Jeanne Mueller and Judith Hale Wood

**What Are You Thankful For?** — 23
    A Multigenerational One-Act Drama For Thanksgiving
        Arthur J. L. Meether

**Thanksgiving For Our Day** — 31
    A Responsive Reading For Thanksgiving
        Judy Gattis Smith

**Recalling Our Blessings** — 35
    An Informal Interactive Children's Moment For Thanksgiving
        Judy Gattis Smith

**Is It Still Wonderful?** — 39
    A Sermon For Thanksgiving
        Louis H. Valbracht

**Welcome The Spirit Of Christmas** — 45
    A Preparation And An Order Of Worship For The Hanging Of The Greens
        Janet Burton

**The Christmas Stranger** — 61
    A Multigenerational Drama For Christmas
        Bill Thomas

**The Christmas Stranger Returns** — 85
    A Multigenerational Drama For Christmas
        Bill Thomas

**A Christmas Remembrance** — 103
    A Multigenerational Christmas Drama With An Order Of Worship
        Arthur J. L. Meether

**Christmas, Then And Now: As Witnessed By The Angels** — 113
    A One-Act Christmas Drama For Adults Or Older Youth
        Robert V. Dodd

**It's So Christmas-See!**    **125**
    A One-Act Modern Christmas Drama
        Myra Shofner

**The Legend Of The North Star (Little Dot Makes A Wish)**    **141**
    A Christmas Story For Children
        Donna J. Fetzer

**The Legend Of The North Star (Little Dot Makes A Wish)**    **147**
    A Christmas Play For Youth Of All Ages
        Donna J. Fetzer

**The Fourth Wise Man**    **155**
    An Epiphany Drama For Adults Or Older Youth
        Adalya Hadar

**Contributors**    **173**

# Come!
# See What
# God Has Done

A Thanksgiving Event For Children

# Jeanne Mueller
and
# Judith Hale Wood

# Contents

| | |
|---|---|
| Introduction | 8 |
| Poster Ideas For Various Centers | 9 |
| Bless This House | 12 |
| Nature's Nook | 14 |
| God Gives; We Give Thanks | 16 |
| Food, Fabulous Food | 18 |
| Friendship And Fun | 20 |
| Wonderfully Made | 21 |

# Introduction

"Come! See What God Has Done" has been designed to make children aware of God's many blessings so often taken for granted. Experiences and activities included in this program focus on families, God's world of nature, our religious heritage, food, friendships and fun times, and our bodies and senses.

A guide sheet for each activity center includes:
1. An activity center title with suggestions for creating an appropriate environment.
2. A scripture verse to be displayed on a tagboard at the activity center.
3. A guided learning experience that provides an opportunity for the children to share their personal thoughts and feelings.
4. Several follow-up activities to choose from according to preference, time schedule, or available materials.
5. A closing prayer to be used with each group at the conclusion of the activity.

This Thanksgiving event was developed to last approximately 75 minutes and to include children in kindergarten through grade six. The time period is adjustable, and older or younger children could be included. Although the Thanksgiving event was designed for use with church school teachers and their children, parents could be invited to attend, thus making it an intergenerational event.

The first hour is spent in ten-minute segments at each of the six activity centers. The final minutes can be a gathering together of the entire group for some singing and a closing prayer.

The Thanksgiving event will function smoothly if each class is grouped together and moves as a class from center to center according to the time allowed.

At the beginning, each child is given a paper turkey without any feathers. As each activity center is completed, the child receives a feather representing that particular activity, which is stapled on his/her turkey. At the end of the event, the turkeys should be complete with feathers.

# Poster Ideas For Various Centers

I

II

**III**

**IV**

V

VI

# Bless This House

**Description of Activity Center**

On poster board, display magazine pictures of families working and playing together.

**Scripture Verse**

*Come and see what God has done: he is awesome in his deeds among mortals.*
— Psalm 66:5

**Guided Learning Experience**

Discuss family life with the children by asking:
1. What are some things families do together?
2. What problems do families sometimes have?
3. What joys do families share?
4. Why do you suppose God gives us families?
5. What is special about your family?

**Follow-up Activities**
**A. Nut Family Plaque**

On a 6" by 8" piece of wood or heavy cardboard, glue a nut (walnut, pecan, almond, hazelnut, peanut) — one for each member of your family. With plastic eyes and bits of material and yarn, decorate nuts to be representative of your family. Add BLESS THIS HOUSE in alphabet cereal or alphabet noodles. Thank God for your family.

## B. Indian Corn and Feather Place Card

Use a 4" by 6" rectangle of paper. Fold in half. Add turkey body, feathers for tail, and a peppercorn for eye. Glue on Indian corn and guest's name.

## C. Thanksgiving Card

Make a Thanksgiving card showing something you are thankful for and add the following verse:

*My dad is good;*
*My mom is kind.*
*They are the best*
*That I'll ever find.*

## Closing Prayer

Our heavenly Father, we thank you for giving us a family.
We thank you for moms who hug us, bake us cookies, and care for us when we are sick.
We thank you for dads who work hard every day, love us, and help us with our homework.
Help us to be a kind and loving member of our family. Amen.

# Nature's Nook

**Description of Activity Center**

Collect and display some pictures showing the beauty of God's natural world. Arrange any of the following for the children to explore: seeds, insects, pine cones, acorns, gourds, pumpkins, Indian corn, thistles, wheat, pods.

**Scripture Verse**

*I will give thanks to the Lord with my whole heart; I will tell of all your wonderful deeds.*
— Psalm 9:1

**Guided Learning Experience**

If you could pick your favorite season, which one would it be? Why?

For the following activity, speak slowly so that the children will have an opportunity to paint a mental picture.

Close your eyes and think about a time in summer when you were so very hot. Your skin was all sticky and sweaty. Then think of how you felt when you jumped into a cool stream of water — how cool you felt.

Now think about wintertime. It has snowed and the tree branches and bushes are covered with snow. Icicles hang from the roof. Your nose and cheeks are so cold that they tingle. You have lots of fun sledding and making snowballs.

Think of autumn. The sun is warm. The leaves on the trees are bright red and yellow. The leaves on the ground rustle as you walk in them. You have raked and raked and have a huge pile of leaves. Then you and a friend jump and roll in the pile of leaves. What fun!

Think of one more season — it's spring. Some days the ground is still frozen and hard. You've seen two birds building a nest in the tree outside your window in preparation for the baby birds soon to come. Pussy willows are in bloom in your yard. And then it happens! One day you see a tiny green shoot appear in the garden. Several days later, there are purple and yellow crocuses blooming in your yard.

Most of the things we have thought about are gifts from God — things that we can't buy, things that God gives us — water, sunshine, birds, and trees.

Can you think of three other things that God gives you that you can't buy?

## Suggested Activities

**A. Thanksgiving Tree**

Draw around your hand three times on colored paper.

Print what you are thankful for on the hands.

Cut out the hands and glue them on the tree.

**B. Nature Collage**

Children combine natural materials to create a collage and add the scripture passage from Psalm 9:1.

**C. Gourd Creatures**

Children can use natural materials like berries, acorns, cranberries, popcorn, dried flowers, as well as markers, feathers, and buttons to create a Gourd Creature.

**Closing Prayer**

God, our Creator, we thank you for the beautiful and wonderful world you have created. Especially we thank you for the seasons, for sunshine and rain, for trees to climb and streams to play in. Help us to care for and wisely use these gifts you have given us. Amen.

# God Gives; We Give Thanks

**Description of Activity Center**

Appropriate items related to this center would include a Bible, the church hymnal, a cross, the communion cup, and bread.

**Scripture Verse**

*Let us come into his presence with thanksgiving; let us make a joyful noise to him with songs of praise!* — Psalm 95:2

**Guided Learning Experience**

Help the children to think about giving and receiving and what God has given to his people.
1. What is the neatest gift you have ever received?
2. What is the nicest gift you have ever given?
3. What do you think is the greatest gift God has ever given?
4. What is the greatest gift you can give God?

Talk with the children about the symbolism and meaning of each of the items displayed.

**Suggested Activities**

**A. Pyramid of Thanks**

In each section of the pyramid, the children should place some thing that reminds them of their religious heritage. Suggestions include a picture of their church, a cross, a Bible, and a picture of Christ. (Pattern for pyramid is included.)

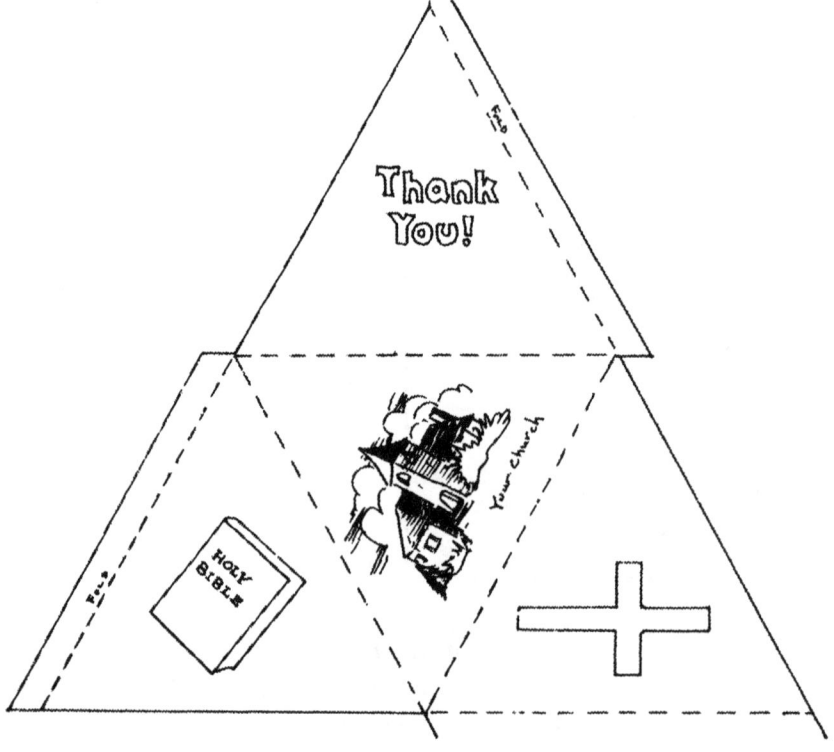

**B. Give Thanks Centerpiece**

Each child traces his/her hand on folded construction paper. Cut them out, leaving the middle fingers attached. Print or have available a copy of the grace printed below to add to the hands. Encourage the use of the grace at mealtime.

*To God who gives us daily bread*
　*A thankful song we raise,*
*And pray that he who sends us food*
　*Will fill our hearts with praise.*

**C. Church Symbol Silhouette**

Cover an area with newspapers. Cut an arch-shaped panel from dark construction paper. Children choose a cardboard pattern of a church, cross, or folded hands. Place the pattern on the paper and, using thinned white poster paint in a spray bottle, "spatter paint" the symbol.

**Closing Prayer**

Loving God, we thank you for our church, for our teachers, and pastor who help us learn about you and your ways, and most of all, for sending us your Son Jesus who taught us to love one another. Help each of us become the best person we can be. Amen.

# Food, Fabulous Food

**Description of Activity Center**

A cornucopia filled with fruits makes an ideal centerpiece for this center.

**Scripture Verse**

*The earth has yielded its increase; God, our God, has blessed us.* — Psalm 67:6

**Guided Learning Experience**

Ask what the cornucopia represents and then begin the conversation about food by asking:
1. What is your favorite place to eat?
2. What is your favorite food?
3. What is the most special meal you can remember?

Listen to this story and be ready to tell how you would feel if you were the mother, the father, or God.

> Once upon a time there was a little girl named Terrible Liz. Her name was Terrible because she was terrible. When she played, she always insisted on her own way. When she left her room, it always looked like a disaster area. If she met you outside she would say, "Where did you get those horrible looking pants?" or "What in the world did you do to your hair?"
>
> But the time she was at her worst was at mealtime. After her dad had worked hard at his job, after Mom had gone grocery shopping and cooked dinner, Terrible Liz could be heard to say, "Oh, no, not that stuff again," or "You know I hate string beans, why do you fix them?" or "Yuck, I'm not eating any squash!" or "Why can't you ever fix something I like?"

Well, that's the way Terrible Liz talked and acted. Let's think about some people that Liz didn't consider.
1. How do you think Mom felt after she had shopped and fixed dinner?
2. Why did Dad go to work?
3. Where did the food come from?
4. What things did Terrible Liz do to show that she wasn't thankful to her parents and to God?

**Suggested Activities**
**A. Turkey Shapes**
Cut turkey shapes from bread with a cookie cutter. Children can spread them with peanut butter. Decorate with raisin eyes and jelly tail feathers.

**B. Harvest Bowl**
Children may help prepare the fruits and mix them.
    2 apples peeled, cored, and diced
    1 bunch of grapes
    2 handfuls of nuts
    2 handfuls of raisins
    2 Tablespoons honey
    granola cereal

Mix fruits and nuts. Add honey. Sprinkle with granola. Scoop into snack-size baggies.

**C. Pilgrim Cornbread**
The Indians introduced corn to the Pilgrims. Cornbread has become a traditional Thanksgiving dish. Bake this ahead of time and offer bite-sized pieces. Distribute copies of the recipe for the families to make at home.
    2 cups cornmeal
    2 teaspoons of baking powder
    1 egg beaten
    1 cup milk
    2 Tablespoons oil
    2 Tablespoons of sugar
    1/2 teaspoon salt

Sift dry ingredients. Add milk, oil, egg, and sugar. Mix well. Pour into greased 8-inch square pan. Bake at 400 degrees for 35 minutes.

**Closing Prayer**
God, our Provider, help us to be thankful for all the food you have given us, not just those foods we like. Help us to remember that there are many in our world who go to bed hungry. We thank you for our food and also for the people who work so that we may eat. Amen.

# Friendship And Fun

**Description of Activity Center**

A collage of children's faces can be displayed with sports equipment, games, and dolls. Add a graffiti board that is titled, A FRIEND IS ... Since this center involves a storytelling experience, plan a special area such as a tent or blanket in a quiet corner.

**Scripture Verse**

*Blessed are the peacemakers, for they will be called children of God.* — Matthew 5:9

**Guided Learning Experience**

Stir up children's thinking by asking:
1. What makes a good friend?
2. What qualities of a good friend do you have?
3. What can you tell about people by just looking at them?

Have children add their own thoughts and feelings to the graffiti board.

**Suggested Activity**

The public library has a wealth of good books/stories about friends and friendship. A highly recommended story with a Thanksgiving theme is *Cranberry Thanksgiving* by Wende and Harry Devlin (New York: Parents Magazine Press, 1971).

*Cranberry Thanksgiving* is a delightful tale of two friends, Maggie and Mr. Whiskers, and a famous cranberry bread recipe. If using this story, be sure to serve some cranberry bread or muffins to the children after the story is told.

**Closing Prayer**

Almighty God, we thank you for all the special friends we have and for the good times we have playing and sharing with our friends. We know so well how we like our friends to treat us. Help us to be patient, kind, and loving, not only to our friends but also to those who are unfriendly toward us. Amen.

# Wonderfully Made

**Description of Activity Center**

Display a large sheet of white mural paper with this adapted verse from Psalm 47:1 — "O, you children, Clap your hands, Praise the Lord!" Children are to paint one of their hands with various colors of poster paint and then press them on the mural paper to make a collage of handprints.

Also display the Wonderfully Made poster, which can be used to introduce the activities.

**Scripture Verse**

*I will give thanks to the Lord with my whole heart.* — Psalm 9:1

**Guided Learning Experience**

See if the children can name their five senses. Ask them to share with one another:
1. The sweetest/foulest smell they have ever smelled.
2. The hottest/coldest thing they have ever felt.
3. The prettiest/ugliest thing they have ever seen.
4. The loudest/softest thing they have ever heard.
5. The best/worst thing they have ever tasted.

God has given us wonderfully created bodies that we often take for granted. Think of how difficult life would be if part of one's body didn't function properly. We should care for our bodies by seeing that we eat properly, exercise regularly, and avoid things (drugs, alcohol, tobacco) that can harm what God has given us.

**Suggested Activities**

Prepare the following "sense testers" for the children to experience and then identify.

**A. Smell**

In small bottles or baby food jars, place cotton balls saturated with several drops of peppermint extract, some peanut butter, coffee, vanilla extract, and vinegar for the children to smell.

**B. Hear**

Record the following sounds for the children to recognize: a zipper, an alarm clock buzzing, a train whistle, and a car motor starting up.

**C. Taste**

Provide each child with a small taste of each of the following to be identified: salt, lemon, banana, celery, and sugar.

### D. Feel

In small paper bags place the following items: some cotton, a spool, a cookie cutter, a sponge, and a rock. Staple the bags shut and number them. Have the children feel the bag and identify the contents.

### Closing Prayer

Dear God, our Creator, you have provided us with a wonderfully made body. Help us to use our mouths to say kind things, to use our hands in loving and helpful ways, to use our eyes to see beauty in your world, and to use our ears to hear pleasant sounds. May our hearts be filled with love and our actions show that we are truly your children. Amen.

# What Are You Thankful For?

A Multigenerational
One-Act Drama For Thanksgiving

## Arthur J. L. Meether

# What Are You Thankful For?

**Characters**
**Grandma Lane** — an elderly lady in her early eighties, now a resident in a nursing home, walks with extreme difficulty
**Trevor Lane** — Grandma Lane's son; husband and father of his own family
**Debbie Lane** — Trevor's wife and mother of the Lane children
**Kevin Lane** — oldest of the Lane children, a high school senior
**Rosemary Lane** — another of the Lane children, a high school sophomore
**Junior (Trevor Jr.) Lane** — third Lane child, a high school freshman
**Randy Lane** — older— of the Lane twins, age ten
**Andy Lane** — Randy's twin, age ten
**Helen Lane** — Trevor's sister, career woman, never married, active in a women's rights movement, age 55
**David Dawson** — Trevor Lane's brother-in-law
**Olivia Dawson** — David's wife (Trevor's sister)
**Chip Dawson** — oldest Dawson child, high school junior
**Charlie Dawson** — middle Dawson child, eighth grader
**Sue Dawson** — youngest Dawson child, age ten

**Props**
Chairs
Sofas

**Time**
Thanksgiving Day

**Setting**
The two families are just returning from church to the Lane home where they plan to have Thanksgiving dinner together.

---

*(Trevor and David enter, helping Grandma Lane to a chair. The rest struggle in and find a place to sit or go about their business.)*

**Debbie:** *(sighs)* Now the work begins. I guess I really don't know if I enjoy Thanksgiving at all with all the work to do.

**Helen:** I think it's time the men did the cooking. I always did say if it was up to the men to have the babies, scrub up the house, and put the food on the table, things would be a lot different. Well, girls, let's get to it.

**Trevor:** I guess, Helen, that is why we men are so *thankful* that God invented women!

*(Debbie, Helen, and Olivia exit; Helen glares back at her brother, but says nothing further.)*

**Junior:** Hey, Dad! Could I put that in my confirmation lesson? That men are thankful that God invented women? The pastor wants us to come up with a list of things we should be thankful for. He says to interview members of our family and find out what they are thankful for.

**Trevor:** Well, Son, I guess you could say that. I doubt if that one item will satisfy the pastor, though. It will be a bit before the ladies get the food on the table. You could interview us all right now.

**Junior:** Great. Can I start with you, Uncle Dave?

**David:** I would sure like to help you, but I was laid off at the factory for two months. Just got called back to work two weeks ago. Those odd jobs I was able to get in between just didn't pay very much. We have had a miserable year. I cannot think of anything to add to your list to be thankful for.

**Junior:** Okay, Uncle Dave, I guess you have had it rough. What about you, Kevin? Can you help me?

**Kevin:** Sorry, little brother. You ought to know better than to ask me. I didn't make either the football or basketball team, and you know how hard I worked for that, but in a big school like ours there is too much competition. Besides, I think the coach is prejudiced. He favors those big guys with well-known names. Then, you know, Nancy dumped me and started going out with my best friend.

**Junior:** Can you help me, Rosemary?

**Rosemary:** With my acne problem, I should be thankful? If I can't get something so that I won't look like I have the measles or chicken pox all the time, I will never find a boyfriend. I will end up an old maid like Aunt Helen. All the other girls have regular boyfriends. Not me.

**Trevor:** God forbid, child! Not like your Aunt Helen.

**Helen:** *(sticks her head in, having heard her name spoken)* Who is talking about me behind my back, as if I didn't know?

**Junior:** Aunt Helen, I need some help with my confirmation lesson. You can surely tell me some things you are thankful for. You just told us last week that you have been made third vice-president of your firm.

**Helen:** *(steps into the room and speaks indignantly)* Tokenism! That is what it is. Do you know that I am the only woman in upper-level management in the firm? *(becomes very bitter)* If I had been a man, I would have gotten my present position years ago. If there had been no sex discrimination, I would be president of the firm by now. As you see, I cannot help you out. I have to get back to the "woman's place" in the kitchen so you men can eat. *(turns to Trevor)* One more wise remark from you, Trevor, and the turkey goes into the garbage can. *(exits)*

*(Olivia looks in to see what is going on just as Helen is about to exit.)*

**Junior:** Aunt Olivia. Do you have a minute? Can you tell me what you are thankful for? It's for my confirmation lesson.

**Olivia:** *(meekly)* I know I should be thankful ... for the sunlight, the air, and all. The catechism says ... Well, I guess I can't quote it anymore. You can look it up. You know what a bad time of it I have had, though: I had that awful operation. I had so much pain. It still bothers me. I was in the hospital for three weeks and our insurance didn't cover all the costs. I can't help you, though, I know I shouldn't talk like this.

**Junior:** *(desperately)* Randy, Andy?

**Randy and Andy:** *(together)* Naw. We got nothing to be thankful about.

**Junior:** Well, Chip?

**Chip:** I'm with Randy and Andy except maybe I ought to be thankful that I don't have a brother who is only thirty minutes younger than I am to get into my hair. But I've got Charlie and he is a real pain.

**Charlie:** I'm not thankful, either, because I got a big bully brother around to make life miserable and push all his work off on me to do, as if I didn't already have enough.

**Andy:** Maybe you could be thankful that you don't have two big bully brothers like Randy and me.

**David:** That will be enough, boys. Anymore of this and no video games for you!

**Junior:** Can you please help me, Sue? At least you don't have acne problems.

**Sue:** Well, I might have. Rosemary told me that I could get it just like she has it because we are cousins and we have the same genes. I worry about it, so I have no time to be happy.

**Junior:** Well, Dad, I guess that leaves it to you.

**Trevor:** I'm going to have to beg off like all the rest. I guess you will just have to tell the pastor that we have had a bad year. As you know, we didn't get rain in time, so the crop yields have been off. Now prices are down, too, while all my costs are way up. Never did get the bill for the last repairs to the tractor, but I know it will be a big one. Next year there will be Kevin's college expenses, then Rosemary's, yours, and so on. I feel, at times, like I have the weight of the world on my back.

**Junior:** Okay, Dad. I will tell the pastor.

**Grandma Lane:** Well, aren't you going to ask me, Junior?

**Junior:** I didn't mean to forget you, Grandma, but I knew that you have a hard time walking and you have to live in that nursing home. I guess I just took it for granted that you would not be able to help me.

**Grandma Lane:** A good reporter doesn't take things like that for granted. When you are 82, a person can feel thankful just to be on her feet. A lot of people up at the home who are much younger than I am are bedridden or confined to a wheelchair.

**Junior:** But your home was so much nicer than that nursing home. I remember how you used to be so proud of your flowers and your garden. Now you can't do that anymore.

**Grandma Lane:** I did enjoy living in my own home, Junior. I am thankful for the time I had there and, if I could, I would go back there tomorrow. But I know I cannot. I can still move about, but I can no longer do everything for myself. I am thankful that there is a nursing home where I can get the care that I need. I am also thankful that I have such a fine, loyal family who comes to see me often and takes me out to church and for special occasions, like today.

**Trevor:** You did always have a way of seeing the bright side of things, Mother.

**Grandma Lane:** That's right, Trevor. You worry about your farm problems. I know things have not been the way they should be and you have had some special problems, but I also know that you have been able to make enough to support your family and save a little toward those special educational expenses. Remember how it was back when your father was farming? He almost had to give it up. Be thankful that you have it better than that, and be thankful that you live in a country where you have a voice in the political process and can work to improve things.

**Junior:** You do look at things in a different way, Grandma.

*(Helen enters as Grandma Lane begins to speak.)*

**Grandma Lane:** That is right. I can even see things that your Uncle Dave and Aunt Olivia could be thankful for if they've a mind to be. You forgot to mention, Dave, that you had those unemployment benefits while you were laid off. I remember as a child when my father was laid off from work, we would have had nothing at all if our relatives had not helped us out. You did get your job back, too. Olivia complains about her operation. She forgets the good health that it has now brought her. We so quickly forget to be thankful for the kind of health care that is available to us. Many people in the world have no medical care available to them at all. There was a time not too many years ago that the technology and knowledge that can heal us today was not available any place, even if you had money.

**Helen:** You were always a regular Pollyanna, Mother. I, for one, do not buy it all. Things aren't as nice as you say.

**Junior:** What's a Pollyanna, Aunt Helen?

**Trevor:** *(sarcastically)* She was a character in a story your Aunt Helen read years ago. Your Aunt Helen took her as her ideal. That is why she is always so cheerful and sees the bright side of everything all the time.

**Helen:** *(glares at Trevor)* Don't listen to your father, Junior. Pollyanna was a character in a story, all right. She was a blubbering idiot who could not see the reality of how cruel and unrewarding life can be, and usually is, in this society of ours.

**Grandma Lane:** Children, I am ashamed of you. God has given us so much. We all have food, clothing, and the resourcefulness to take care of all our needs. We have our freedom and our personal rights are guarded. We have wonderful schools and the freedom to obtain an education. We should thank God for our superb hospitals and skilled physicians to care for us when we are sick. I expect that they will even be able to solve the problem of acne, given a little time. I could go on — it may seem Pollyanna to you, Helen, but even you have to admit that progress has been made in female rights. I am really ashamed of all of you. Only this morning the pastor preached his sermon on the text of the ten lepers who were made clean. You must not have heard him because you — my own family — sound so much like the nine lepers who could think of no reason to come back and say, "Thank you," for being healed.

**Trevor:** You are right, Mother. We all have so much to be thankful for to God. We have received so much that we take all these good things for granted and get hung up on our petty problems. I see Debbie is motioning us to come to the table. Let's go and really celebrate our thankfulness to God.

*(All exit. Trevor and David help Grandma Lane.)*

# Thanksgiving For Our Day

A Responsive Reading
For Thanksgiving

## Judy Gattis Smith

# Thanksgiving For Our Day

**Instructions**

Decide how you want to present this reading. One or more children or youth may read the Reader part. The entire congregation or a speaking choir may read the Congregation part. Think about your particular group and be creative.

| | |
|---|---|
| Reader: | It isn't easy to always give thanks to God. Sometimes life becomes boring — getting up, going to school, doing homework, goofing off. |
| **Congregation:** | **Nevertheless — there is meaning and possibility and new creation in every day.** |
| Reader: | Sometimes we just feel blah. We don't know the heights of gladness or the depths of agony. |
| **Congregation:** | **Nevertheless — there is tremendous and fascinating mystery in life and in God.** |
| Reader: | We make so many stupid mistakes — always doing and saying the wrong things. |
| **Congregation:** | **Nevertheless — God receives these things, exposes them to God's energies, and offers us back new possibilities.** |
| Reader: | I don't like to read about all the things happening in the world: killings and war and sorrow. |
| **Congregation:** | **Nevertheless — humanity is even now being redeemed. Eternity is united with the present moment, and we are a part of it.** |
| Reader: | But I'm just one child (youth). It seems impossible for me to do anything. |
| **Congregation:** | **Nevertheless — God uses us to bring about his purposes. God's word has been spoken in us and to us. With amazement, ecstasy, and joy, we are confronted by God.** |
| Reader: | Living is an act of faith, then. |
| **Congregation:** | **Living means knowing and participating in the pain and sorrow of life, the confusion, the disappointments, and the frustrations, but saying, "Nevertheless" — and giving thanks.** |

# Recalling Our Blessings

## An Informal Interactive Children's Moment For Thanksgiving

### Judy Gattis Smith

# Recalling Our Blessings

**Props**
Yellow poster board
Green poster board
Red poster board
Orange poster board
White poster board
Blue poster board

**Leader:** Sometimes we do not give thanks to God because we forget God's many blessings to us. Let us use color now to remind us of the many things we have for which to thank God.

*(A child comes forward, carrying a large yellow poster board and stands beside Leader.)*

**Leader:** Think of all the things we have to be thankful for that are yellow. Call out to me some of these things.

*(Congregation responds with words such as: sun, buttercups, butterflies, lemon pie, yellow dress, flame of a candle, canaries, and so on.)*

**Leader:** *(gathers up these words in a simple prayer such as the following)* O God, we do thank thee for the sun and the buttercups, the canaries and the candles, our favorite dress and lemon pies, and for the blessings you have given us that are yellow. Amen.

*(A child comes forward, carrying a green poster board.)*

**Leader:** Let us think now of all the blessings we have that are green.

*(Again, congregation suggests words that make up the prayer. Some examples for green are: grass, trees, pickles, moss, grapes, green beans. The same procedure is carried out for red, orange, white, and yellow. After all the blessings have been received and all the thanks have been expressed in prayer, Leader ends with the following.)*

**Leader:** Will all the children carrying poster boards come forward now? We thank you, God, who has given us so much and placed us in a rainbow world full of your blessings. Amen.

**Hymn:** "All Things Bright And Beautiful"

# Is It Still Wonderful?

A Sermon For Thanksgiving

# Louis H. Valbracht

# Is It Still Wonderful?

Somehow, somebody always does it before each holiday, and so the man in the restaurant asked me the other day, "Well, pastor, what are you going to preach about on Thanksgiving?" And, as always, I was tempted to answer, "I don't know. What would *you* preach about?" Oh, I could help him out by giving him the accepted pattern, the outline that has been hallowed by constant use over the years, revered by redundant repetition.

You always start out somewhere on the rock-ribbed coast of Massachusetts, the bare and bent arm of New England, the white coast of Plymouth. You tell about the little group of religious refugees who landed there 350 years ago. They were blown off course. They thought they would land in Virginia, but there they were on that unfriendly coast. You twang the heartstrings of the congregation by telling them that in the next five months over half of the 101 settlers were in their graves. They had died during the unspeakable hardships and famine and disease in that first, terrible winter, and their graves were left unmarked because the settlers didn't want the Indians to know how many had died.

You tell how, in the spring, when the *Mayflower* set sail again back to the comforts of England and home, not one of the survivors chickened out and went back with the ship. And so you speak of their courage and their devotion and their determination, which are written in the *Mayflower Compact* and would become the life-breath of a great nation. You dwell a while on our national heritage and how we all should congratulate ourselves that we were smart enough to be born Americans. Then you tell how the settlers, after another summer of indescribable hardship, were led by Elder Brewster through the cornfields of Plymouth, and they raised their voices in the ancient song of the psalmist, "The earth is the Lord's and the fullness thereof, the world and they that dwell therein." Then you talk about the wonderful sense of gratitude on the part of the pilgrims.

Then, in order to make the sermon timely and contemporary and relevant — and we are always under a great burden today to make our sermons relevant — you quickly establish your thesis. It goes something like this: If the poor pilgrims could be thankful for just hanging on to dear life, then we ought to be thankful for the affluent American way of life that they founded for us. You search through the newspapers and magazines for choice examples of the thing for which we ought to be thankful. In the magazine section of the newspaper, we may have been told that we could certainly be thankful for the fact that at the turn of the century only a very wealthy family in America could afford a turkey for Thanksgiving because it cost about thirty gold 100-cent Republican dollars. I believe that today most local grocery stores sell oven-ready, corn-fed, vitamins added, self-basting, double-breasted turkeys for about 89 cents a pound.

Togetherness on Thanksgiving costs less, and we should be thankful for that. A person in Washington, for instance, can visit his family in New York on less than $100 travel cost, which the same trip by stagecoach, just a few years back, would cost $1,200 tourist class, federal tax not included.

All of us who are 45 years of age or older can be thankful for the fact that we are here to celebrate Thanksgiving, because a few decades ago, our life expectancy would only have been about 43 years, and most of us wouldn't be around to eat our turkey.

In a previous year's night-before-Thanksgiving tribute, the ladies of Des Moines, Iowa — God bless them — told what they could be thankful for. One housewife was thankful for the fact that this year she had a real roaster in which to do her bird, after 22 years of doing it in the cake pan and having to clean up the oven afterward. Another lady was thankful for the nice weather that she was having, but she said she was glad we had at least one hard freeze that killed all the flowers outside so she could go and buy chrysanthemums at the florists for her table without feeling guilty. One grandmother was thankful for the fact that today's turkeys are all plucked and clean shaven, because in her day she had to pick out all the pin feathers. One career girl in Des Moines was happy because the high boots that are fashionable kept her feet warm, the bulky knit sweaters kept her top warm, and the new-style pantyhose made her knees look better. A mother was thankful for the pebble pattern floor tile they now had in their house that didn't show the dirty marks of little feet. Another mother was thankful for the fact that they now had a protective spray for upholstery because they eat their meals before the television set.

Then you save a few earth-shaking blockbusters to wind up the whole thing, like the fact that while the ration of the pilgrims in the first dreaded winter in Plymouth was only five grains of corn per meal, the state of Iowa alone harvests a billion dollar corn crop.

Well, anyway, the point is made, the thesis is clinched, the sermon is over. Now go home and be thankful, at least for the rest of the day, or shame on you! That's the pattern. That's the accepted pattern! Does anyone want to preach the sermon?

One of the last times I flew to Chicago, I heard a Thanksgiving sermon. It was delivered by a mother in the seat behind me just before we arrived in Chicago. She was giving instructions to an eight-year-old boy, "Now, don't forget when we meet Aunt Helen, don't make me tell you to kiss her and don't make her ask you to." "Oh, Mom!" "Don't forget that Aunt Helen always remembers you on Christmas and your birthday and many other times. She gives you nice things." "Yes, I know, but do I have to *kiss* her? Golly!" So, you see, the outcome of that Thanksgiving sermon was pretty much like the outcome of most Thanksgiving sermons — if you're thankful, you don't need a sermon; and if you aren't, no sermon is very convincing.

That's my problem. I've pondered it for some time now, and, strangely enough, I was thinking about it last week driving over to a college football game. We drove by one great field after another. In the back of my mind there came the words and the tune of an old anthem we used to sing. That anthem and the tune of it kept running through my mind like a broken record. Somehow, I've been humming it all week: "The valley stands so thick with corn that they laugh and sing." I have finally decided the thing that was beating my consciousness was the sheer, unspeakable, unbelievable *wonder* of the field that was stretching out all around us as far as the eye could see. I knew it stretched for hundreds of miles in every direction. The sheer weight and bulk of the miracle was before our eyes! And if, somehow, I could catch the wonder of the miracle that was there in front of us, it would make the so-called miraculous feeding of the 5,000 look like a light afternoon tea.

The simple fact was that in about 130 days those fields had gone from black, barren soil to this miracle! The Bible speaks of harvesting grain a hundredfold. I picked up one of the ears of corn that we were using for decoration. How much was this? I've never been able to get the information from a farmer, so I counted the kernels myself. There are 864 kernels on an ear of corn. That one seed has reproduced itself, not one hundredfold, but 864 times!

What about the rest of it — the root, the stalk, the leaves, the tassel? I sought for information and, again, I had difficulty finding it. Finally, I got my answer from a fertilizer salesman. He tells me that in fodder alone, on the average cornfield, there is 30,000 pounds of fodder per acre. Boiling that down to its simplest terms on an average farm of 300 acres of corn, there would be one million pounds of food and other valuable materials that had not been there eighteen weeks before. One *million* pounds of it! Do you catch the earth-shaking wonder of it?

If we did, then we wouldn't, for one minute, listen to some supposedly intelligent scholar or scientist who stands up on his pip-squeak hind legs and tells us with pompous profundity that this whole thing is a combination of the accidental evolvement of an accidental universe, assisted by the technological skills and scientific advances of an accidentally evolving human mind. You would, instead, see him for the eloquent, if articulate, *fool* that he is!

If a person, inspired by this one million pounds of foodstuff, inspired by the goodness of God at this miracle, is hopelessly, provincially naive, then the man who doesn't see this miracle as a miracle of the grace of God — no matter how sophisticatedly brilliant he might be — is a blind, unmitigated fool! Why don't we call them "fools"? They are, you know, and we take them so seriously, as though their word were law. I don't care how many degrees they print after their names. They are ignorant, stupid, blind fools. And it's about time we woke up to the fact.

You see, what we lost and are losing is the sheer wonder of God's grace. Again and again in the gospel narrative, that word is used to describe the revelation of God in Jesus Christ. They *wondered* at what they saw. They *wondered* at his words. They were filled with *wonder* in his presence. It was sheer, joyous wonder that provoked the words of the old anthem that I had been humming, which, incidentally, came from Psalm 65: "The pastures are clothed with flocks, the valleys also are covered over with corn. They shout for joy; they also sing." Thanksgiving is not and can never be a strained, contrived, documented, intellectually established frame of mind. It is a joyous explosion! It's a shout of wonder at the grace of God! You see, that's our problem. Today we have miracles on every street corner, in every kitchen, in every factory, in every garage. We are blasé and jaded and bored by miracles. We have lost our wonder at them.

How can a bored heart overflow with spontaneous joy? Isn't it rather strange that in an age of wonder we have lost our capacity to wonder? How long since you were filled with awe at some ineffable mystery? "Wonderful" is one of the most overworked words in our vocabulary. It falls glibly from every lip, before every situation, on every subject, until it has the hollow ring of insincerity. Obviously, if *everything* is wonderful, then *nothing* is wonderful. This is what we need to remember. At a tender age, our children learn the trick of affecting a bored sophistication about everything. Oh, it's all quite wonderful — but they aren't impressed!

How many variations of the "shaggy dog" story are there? Is it the one where the stranger walks into the village store and sees a man and a large dog seated at a table playing checkers? The stranger watches in stunned fascination, while the dog, with keen skill and cunning strategy, bests his man opponent and wins the checker game. Finally, the stranger blurts out, "That's so wonderful!" The man replies, "What's so wonderful about it? I beat him two out of three." How many variations of that story do we have, just to point out the fact that nothing is miraculous, that nothing is wonderful? We're not moved by anything.

Socrates said it, "Wonder is the feeling of the philosopher." Philosophy begins with wonder, with the open, curious, and childlike mind.

Rachel Carson in her book, *The Sea Around Us*, tells about taking a two-year-old nephew to see the ocean for the first time. She was reminded of the child's world, full of wonder and excitement, fresh and new and beautiful. She expresses her wish for every child that they might have a sense of wonder so indestructible that it would last throughout life, an unfailing antidote for the boredom and disenchantments of later years.

One hundred and fifty years ago, Wordsworth saw the same dulling imprisonment that enslaved the adult mind:

*Trailing clouds of glory we do come from God who is our home.*
*Heaven lies about us in our infancy.*
*Whither has the glory and the dream?*
*At length the man perceives it die away*
*And fade into the life of dull and common day.*

How sad it is that life goes that way, that nothing is left to the imagination. Man no longer wonders. He supposedly knows.

But Browning writes:

*The wise thrust sings his song twice over*
*Lest you think he never could recapture,*
*That first, wild, careless rapture.*

That's what we've lost, isn't it? We are such a dull people — bored, unmoved, unexcited, and boring. That's at the heart of our society. We bore each other. We no longer have cause for song. Life is just an old chorus, an overplayed, scratchy record, monotonous, repetitious. Long ago we lost our first, wild, careless rapture at the sheer fact of living! Pragmatic education in our day has, as its prime purpose, the equipping of a child with the skills necessary to cope with the pressing affairs of a practical age. Knowledge is a tool for manufacturing dollar bills. That's important, isn't it? We teach good, solid, practical subjects like how to park a car properly, or how to make do-it-yourself repairs on the garbage disposal. Where is the possibility of beauty, of joy, of rapture, of awe, of wonder? You don't get paid for those, do you, so what good are they? A rose is not a crimson petal upon which the drops of clear, morning dew reflect the blue of the sky. A rose is a rose, botanically related to the wild briar. We've got answers for everything, haven't we?

Perhaps only our age could produce the young woman who said to me just the other day, "I come to church to hear a sermon, which I hope will be an interesting discussion of some practical problem. Why do you have to louse it up with all of that other junk?" Of course, "the other junk" to which she referred was the liturgy, the hymns, the confession, and the prayers. I feel sorry for such a person, for they, obviously, have never experienced the greatest experience in life — the height that the human spirit can reach, the awe and wonder of worship.

Do you think you could actually celebrate a Thanksgiving Day in any way except by congregational worship? Be assured, there is no other way. Our hymns, our anthems, our symbolism — all of the symbolism of our worship — are the attempts that we make to say something that cannot be put into mere words. We sing because we can't say certain things. They don't come out right. They sound correct only in song. They express our wonder at the love, the goodness, the miraculous grace of God; and, we must do it together. There is no occasion for private worship. We must express our awe and wonder and thanksgiving.

"The valley stands so thick with corn; the hills also are covered with flocks. They *shout* for joy! They *laugh*! They *sing*!" That, beloved, is thanksgiving. Do you feel it?

# Welcome The Spirit Of Christmas

## A Preparation And An Order Of Worship For The Hanging Of The Greens

### Janet Burton

**Preparation**

# Welcome The Spirit Of Christmas

Churches can begin the tradition of hanging the greens with a very small investment. A modest nest egg can be hatched into a very satisfying event when a handful of creative people incubate it. Here are the basic elements for beginning.

**The Greens**

As the name tells us, we hang evergreens (and other appropriate decorations we may choose to add to them) to enhance our holiday worship events. Garlands, wreaths, and sprays are the beginning place. These can be either artificial or natural greens, and a good case can be made for each. Some advantages of the artificial greens are: 1) fire safety, 2) their reusability, and 3) convenience.

Every worship room is unique and offers wonderfully creative opportunities to decorate. Think about wreaths and garlands for the platform area: railings around the choir, instrument boxes, baptistry. Lovely sprays might be added high on either side of the front. Festive matching bows will tie these together by color and design. Later, doves, poinsettias, or silk ornaments could be added to the greens. Already the room looks beautiful! When members with actual floral arranging skills come into the picture, a wonderland can result. Balconies, windows, pews, doorways, and aisles can be included.

**Advent Wreath**

One way to add interaction between congregation and worship leaders during the four Sundays leading up to Christmas is by having an Advent wreath. Traditionally this is an 18- to 24-inch evergreen wreath laid flat on or near the remembrance table, with four colored candles standing evenly spaced within it, and a larger, white Christ Candle in the center. A candle is lighted each week to "count down" the weeks of Advent, so that on the first Sunday only one candle is lighted, on the second Sunday two are lighted, and so on.

Each candle is assigned a significance, such as the Candle of Hope, the Candle of Joy, the Candle of Peace, and the Candle of Love. Families and individuals may take turns lighting the candles each Sunday during worship. The large Christ Candle is lighted Christmas Eve or Christmas morning when the congregation gathers.

As an alternative to the evergreen wreath, five large candles (four colored and one white) can be placed at varying heights on the draped remembrance table. It is effective to use brass candleholders with these, and satin or velvet are attractive fabrics for a drape. A poinsettia, evergreen spray, large Bible, or Nativity figures may also be added. You will find the Advent wreath or candles called for in all of the programs in this book.

**Christmas Tree**

A stately tree adds a focal point to the room. Sometimes it is tasteful to keep the tree a little sophisticated by using only white lights and gold or white decorations. The tree does not have to be very large and showy. A smaller tree (perhaps six to eight feet tall) can be put on a small covered platform to give it necessary height. Carry the spiritual themes of Christmas onto the tree with doves, Chrismons or Nativity symbols, and matching bows. The tree is a perfect illustration of how congregations can begin simply and add to the collection each year. Members with a creative bent would love a Chrismon workshop at some convenient time in the future — something we will talk more about in this chapter.

### Other Decorations

As hanging the greens catches on, you will think of other items that can be added to the collection. Joyful worship banners, bright poinsettias in festive wraps, a set of Nativity figures (we chose one the children could handle freely), and votive candles are examples. If money for decorating is limited (a certain bet in most congregations!), Sunday school classes or other groups in the congregation might contribute modest amounts, especially as they see the tradition growing.

### Music

This is what turns the occasion from a decorating party into a worship experience. Sometimes hanging the greens is more like a musical event or choir recital, with decorating woven throughout the program. Sometimes it is more like a decorating party, with times of reflection created by congregational singing and special presentations. Variation from year to year increases the congregation's interest. The key word here is cooperation. Ministers, musicians, laypersons, and artists all combine to make an event that glorifies God and delights worshipers.

### The Children

Focus especially on the children and youth of the church family. Include them in several ways. In fact, make them the stars — give them the best seats. What a wonderful way to communicate Bible truths and valued traditions to the emerging congregation! Invite them to sing, to decorate the tree, to come onto the platform with the pastor for the reading of the Christmas story from the Bible. Take time in Sunday school to help them make Chrismons for the tree. Choose them for candlelighters. Plan a family fellowship after hanging the greens with child-friendly refreshments and goodie sacks. Build memories and faith in the children of the congregation. Make it fun!

### Drama

It's the icing on the cake! Bring in Bible persons from Nativity stories and the adventure becomes almost mystical. Invite a couple of angels and the event takes on a life of its own. Drama workshops can begin by researching Nativity narratives in the prophets and the gospels. While dramas may take some license to create contexts or elaborate on the scriptures, they must remain true to the known facts in every way. One trained drama coach will help immensely here.

Bring it all together, and once you have experienced it, Christmas will never be the same without hanging the greens!

## Planning For Creative Workshops

We are all creative beings, made in the image of a Creator God. Creating is enjoyable, affirming, inspiring, spending valuable time together, watching and helping as imaginations come to life. Relationships develop as creations evolve. Here are five ideas for workshops that will enhance

Christmas worship and hanging the greens if you choose to try it in your church. (They do not have to all be done in the same year.)

**Banner Making**

Invite those who enjoy design, stitchery, quilting, and fabric art to put their heads together and come up with a set of Christmas worship banners. One nice set can be used for years, and the investment can be quite reasonable. Choose a theme, such as the names for Jesus in the Christmas stories (Jesus, Savior, Only Begotten Son, Immanuel, Prince of Peace, Wonderful Counselor, Mighty God, Everlasting Father). Select a Chrismon symbol to illustrate each, and transpose that onto handmade, matching banners of felt, taffeta, or satin.

Affix a T-shaped pole to each banner so it can be easily carried and positioned. Decide on the locations for hanging banners. Install fasteners on which to hang the banners. Good locations may be found on walls, beams and pillars, or balcony rails. Wonderful banner books are available in Christian bookstores that detail this kind of project, and one of these would be a worthwhile investment for beginners. An entire hanging the greens program can be built around the presentation of the banners.

**Music Rehearsals**

The possibilities here are limited only by the availability of the choral director. Choirs, ensembles, instrumental groups, or soloists can select and prepare music to make hanging the greens truly a worship celebration. Visualize handbells ringing, harps and flutes playing, children's choirs performing, all to the glory of God in the joy of the season. In some churches the adult choir or the youth choir is the loft choir for this service, freeing the sanctuary choir to work on the cantata or musical extravaganza planned for another date.

Include the choral director early in planning stages, so that music selected can enhance the theme of the program. Often anthems and special music being prepared for other worship events of the season can be used in this program also — an important economy in such a busy month.

Many suggestions for congregational songs, carols, and praise songs and for special music presentations are made throughout this book. Congregations have widely varied preferences and resources, and music leaders will want to substitute other music when it would fit their needs better. Music should enhance the theme of the event as much as possible.

**Chrismon Making**

The many ancient and modern Christian symbols or monograms (hence Chrismons) for God are illustrated in banner-making books, also. Some are Greek letters like the Alpha and Omega, which have stood for the names and attributes of God for centuries. Others are pictographs like the dove, the fish, a star, a manger, a lamp. You will need to purchase a set of Chrismon patterns.*

Chrismons are made into Christmas tree ornaments in many ways. Children can use thin styrofoam (cut by adults using a hot wire) into Chrismon shapes, and decorate them with glitter, beads, and sequins. Silk Christmas balls look lovely enhanced with beads, sequins, and braids in Chrismon designs. Felt or fabric can be cut into Chrismon shapes, sewn, stuffed with polyfill and decorated. These are among the easiest kinds to make, and all will last for years if carefully stored.

**Floral Arranging**

While lovely wreaths, garlands, and sprays may be purchased at craft and discount centers, they are made lovelier by experienced hands. A benefit of creative workshops is that those who know how can pass on their knowledge to willing beginners, and these skills will be useful all year long. Consider having an expert floral arranger come and guide a group of your willing members in making matching arrangements and bows for your auditorium worship area.

### A Checklist For Hanging The Greens

Getting from enthusiastic ideas to a well-organized worship event requires a series of intentional steps. One plan of action follows.

**1. Coordinate With Your Ministers**

Laypersons who initiate an idea such as hanging the greens will want to begin by sharing with those who plan worship and family events. If the idea is well received, set a date and time on the approved church calendar. We prefer the first Sunday evening of Advent, which is usually the Sunday following Thanksgiving. (It is helpful to discuss whether the decorations will be disturbed — "undecorated" if you will — for weddings, funerals, or other scheduled worship and music events which occur in December.) Hanging the greens can happen during evening worship or perhaps before or after that hour.

**2. Select A Theme Or Program**

Coordination of decorations, music, and drama will be better if everyone knows in advance what the flavor and purpose of the event will be. Programs like the one following this section are a possible beginning place. If this is a new venture for your church, consider using a rather traditional service. This will provide a better opportunity for the congregation to become educated about the meanings of this tradition.

**3. Enlist A Leadership Team**

Enthusiasm, participation, and ideas are fostered by shared leadership. The person designated as the primary (coordinating) leader will benefit from enlisting a skilled person to be in charge of decorations, another for music, another for program or drama, and perhaps a fourth person to plan a fellowship after the event. Let these people form a planning committee for the event.

**4. Prepare The Script**

Any program chosen will have to be adapted to your own congregation's needs. The architecture of the worship room, the available resources, budget, time, and other constraints will dictate changes. Work through the program with your committee and musicians. When you are satisfied, have your complete script printed for everyone on the planning group.

**5. Schedule Workshops**

If you plan to involve church members in creativity like banner and Chrismon making, drama, music, or floral arranging, schedule working sessions. (It may take three or four work sessions for each of these groups to complete their work.) Allow enough lead time to promote these in the congregation, so that those who are interested will not miss the opportunity.

You will immediately see that these workshops are a natural way to draw in peripheral members and nonmember friends. The fellowship of working with others may help bring them into the church family and the kingdom. Send invitations to recent visitors and absentee members. Make a list of members with a creative bent, and make personal phone calls to ask for their help. Workshops can have many rewarding spin-offs.

### 6. Budget And Purchase Needed Supplies

Remember, it may be well to begin simply and add to the event each year. The evergreens are the first items to buy. If there are no funds for making Chrismons the first year, ask each family to bring one or two favorite ornaments for a "Friendship" tree representative of the congregation.

### 7. Let The Creativity Happen

Gently guide the workshops, and delight in how the combined creativity of members and friends blossoms into unique love gifts to the Lord. The coordinating leader will keep things moving along and affirm others as things progress toward completion.

### 8. Stay In Touch With Ministers

Plans and ideas have a way of evolving. Keep communication frequent and open. Be flexible when changes are needed. Focus on bringing joy to the congregation and glory to the Lord in all areas of the event.

If there is to be a printed program, put all necessary information in the hands of the secretary or typist in ample time.

### 9. Schedule Time To Prepare The Worship Room

On the day of hanging the greens, time is needed actually to get all the decorations, drama props, microphones, and other equipment out and in place. The planning committee and a handyman or custodian comprise the workforce.

Our preference is to spend about two hours in the afternoon (following morning worship, if this takes place Sunday evening). Place garlands, sprays, and wreaths on the floor, just below where they will be hung. Place the hooks or nails that will hold them into walls or rails, each with an ornament wire attached, so members can easily and quickly place greens at the appropriate time in the service. It may be possible to do some of these details the week prior, taking part of the work load off the actual day of the event.

If written assignments to families or team leaders will be needed during the service, prepare these ahead. (See "Hanging The Greens Assignment Sheet" illustration at the end of this chapter.) Put lights on the Christmas tree, attach an extension cord, and try them out. Place ornaments near the tree at "child level" with hanger wires attached. Have the ladder nearby so older children can climb up to decorate higher branches.

When fresh poinsettias are to be used, be sure they are dressed in protective jackets so moisture will not mar the furnishings. If candles are called for, have a lighter or matches ready, and check wicks. *Carefully read over the program script again and list every detail that needs your attention.* It will be time well spent.

**10. Host Hanging The Greens In A Spirit Of Joy**

In all the fuss and fun of preparing, set a spirit of joy that will be caught by worshipers. All the hours of work are lost if a fussy spirit prevails. It may be wise for the coordinating leader not to be an "up-front" platform personality. In this way he or she can move quietly among the worshipers to answer questions and keep things on schedule. It is more important for the congregation to feel happy with what they accomplish, than for every bow to be in place. Garlands, bows, and decorations can be adjusted tomorrow.

**11. Be Available During The Season**

Touch-ups will be needed, especially if some decorations have to be removed for other events. Keep a happy spirit — it's almost fun to get to redo things a time or two or three. (Sometimes church leaders request that other events incorporate and enjoy the worship room decorations during the holidays and leave them undisturbed. This differs from church to church.)

Let your final act be that of writing or phoning a message of thanks to all who helped make the event successful.

---

*CSS Publishing Company has two resources that include patterns for Chrismons: *A Chrismon Service* by Ellen and James Edgar, ISBN 0-89536-500-6; and *Chrismons — They Point To Jesus* by Diane L. Gibson, ISBN 0-7880-0849-8.

# Hanging The Greens Assignment Sheet

**Note To Team Leaders**

We will divide the auditorium into eight work areas as numbered on the following sketch. You will be the leader of everyone sitting in your area. Your team's assignment is circled on the list below.

Your second assignment is to help when the children decorate the Christmas tree. When it is time, gather up all the children in your section (with enough moms and dads to help) and take them to the tree. Let each child put one or more ornaments on the tree.

## Teams And Assignments

**Team 1:** Hang garlands around the piano box railing and hang spray above piano. (Nails are in place.)

**Team 2:** Hang garlands around the organ box railing and hang spray above organ. (Nails are in place.)

**Team 3:** Hang three wreaths on the east auditorium wall. (Nails are in place.)

**Team 4:** Hang two garlands and bows over SE entry door (D-4) as shown in the sketch.

**Team 5:** Hang two garlands and bows over NE entry door (D-1) as shown in the sketch.

**Team 6:** Hang three wreaths on west auditorium wall. (Nails are in place.)

**Team 7:** Hang two garlands and bows over north entry door (D-2) as shown in the sketch.

**Team 8:** Hang two garlands and bows over NW entry door (D-3) as shown in the sketch.

## Note About Doorway Garlands

Note that three nails are already in place at top center and corners of door frame. Begin both garlands at top center, and drape one toward each corner and down the side of the door, using corner nails as holders. You will find ornament wires on nails and on backs of bows to help you fasten garlands securely.

---

Create your copy of pages 53 and 54 as a one-page handout for your team leaders.

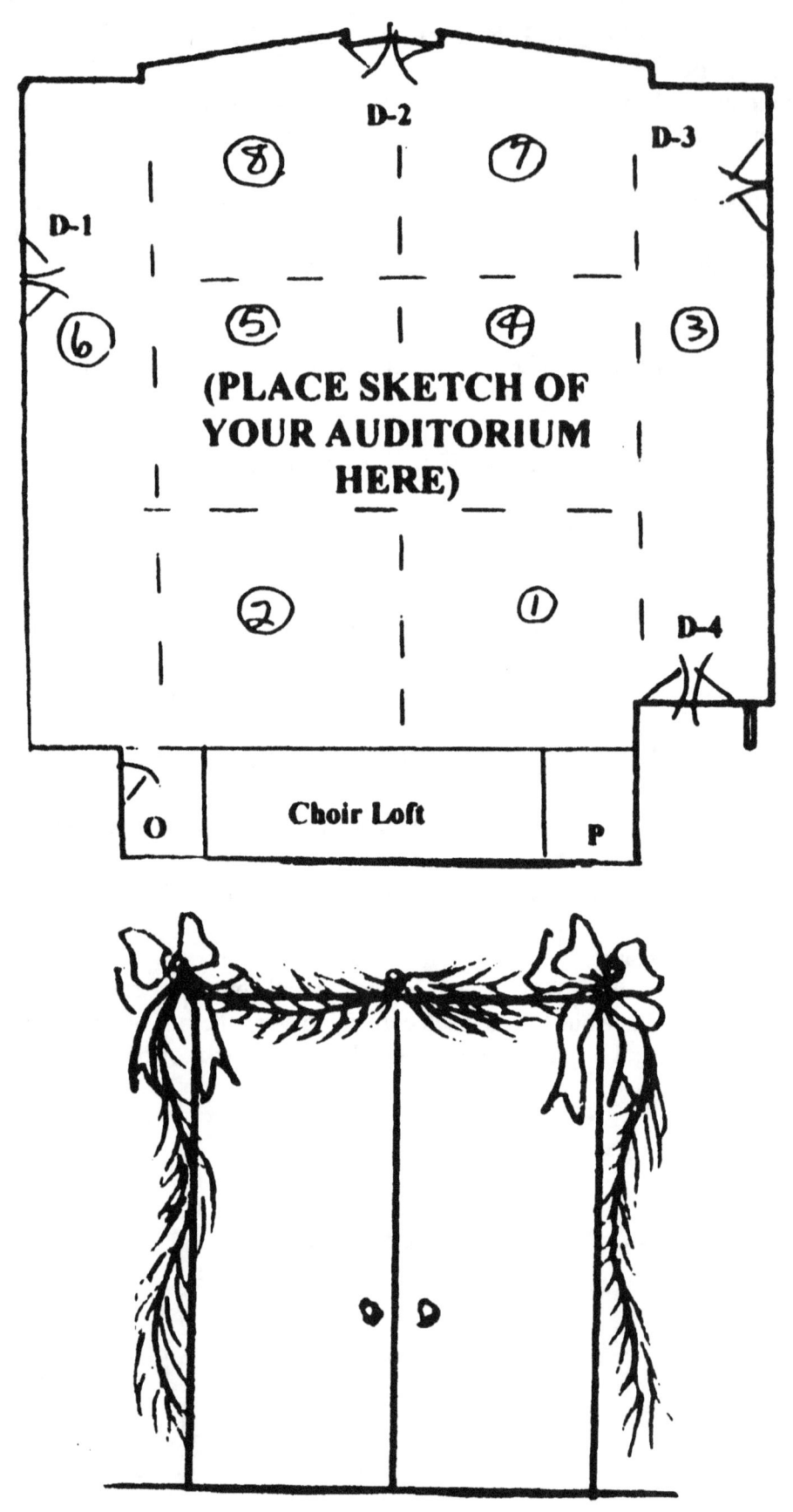

**Order Of Worship**

# Welcome The Spirit Of Christmas

**Description Of This Program**

Visualize the true spirit of Christmas by adding lovely white doves and white poinsettias to the traditional hanging the greens decor. Families can each contribute one or two ornaments from their personal collections to create a "Spirit of Sharing" tree.

**Characters Needed**

**Narrator** — may read all the explanations and direct the decorating
**Minister** — reads some narrations and the Bible passages throughout
**Choral Director** — arranges and leads congregational and special music
**Volunteer Families** — four to eight families who will hang portions of the evergreens

**Preparations**

Carefully make a detailed list of the usual preparations for hanging the greens. The choices you make in decorations will indicate how this program needs to be adapted for your congregation.

Each year your church may want to add something to the collection of available decorations. This year's suggested purchase is white doves. You will need one for each wreath and each garland bow plus one or more for the Christmas tree. Plan for one larger dove to top the tree. A dozen others could be used with the decorations, scattered throughout the boughs.

Purchase enough ribbon to make new bows. Bows of gold net, or gold and white fabric, would complement the white doves. Light blue or another pastel is also a good choice. Two kinds of ribbon, such as a gold lamé and a gold and pastel tapestry, can be used together by someone with floral skills.

When using white doves, we chose also white poinsettias. These are more delicate than the traditional red flowers and will require more tending and careful watering during the month. If they are your choice, plan to have someone carry the plants to a room with natural light and climate control on weekdays unless your worship room has those features. When flower funds are low, consider inviting families in the church to purchase a poinsettia in honor or memory of someone, or asking classes to purchase plants that will later be taken to homebound members. The list of those so honored may be printed in one of the church's publications during the season.

If a "Spirit of Sharing" tree fits into your plans, announce about three Sundays in advance of the program that each family is invited to bring two ornaments from their personal collections for the tree. It is possible to return these after Christmas by putting them in baskets and letting members come to an announced location to reclaim their own. Remember to have extra ornament wires on hand for the hanging the greens event.

Prepare the assignment sheet (on page 53 and 54) for each of the families that will hang the greens, so they understand just what part of the decorating falls to them. Also enlist people to light the Advent candle and others to carry banners. Note that the poinsettias may be brought by those who purchased them. Enlist a group to bring votive candles, and make necessary arrangements for someone to help them light their candles just before they are brought to the worship area.

**Music**

Quiet background music, simple carols, and worship choruses are suggested, with two special music offerings, which you may substitute for your choice. This is a good program for a busy year when the choirs are involved in other pursuits and time to work on music is limited.

## Order Of Program

**Quiet Music:** "Sweet, Sweet Spirit"

*(Minister welcomes everyone warmly and asks that families sit together during the singing of the first song, so that family groups can work as units during the evening. Add that "family" in the church always refers to any kind of grouping: single parents with children, empty nesters, families with three or four generations represented, groups of single friends, or parents with children. Encourage families to "adopt" people near them who are without family in the service.)*

**Congregational Song:** "The Family Of God"

**Prayer:** (by Minister)

### I. The Spirit Of Hope: Lighting The Advent Candle

**Narrator:** Each year about this time we hear people say, "I haven't got the Christmas spirit yet," or "I just can't seem to get the Christmas spirit this year." It takes a while — some years longer than others. But eventually, as we hear the carols on radios and department store intercoms, and see the tinseled trees and counters bulging with gift suggestions, we begin to recapture the feelings of Christmases past and the spirit returns.

As Christians we look for something more in Christmas than these material and tangible offerings: something deeper — a touchback to the original event — a spirit of hope from God's own heart. Walking through Christmas on Main Street, we miss the hope of the season — the promise of a precious Savior Son who would become the Lamb of God, sent to take away the sins of the world. This hope is the core of the Christmas spirit for us who believe.

**Minister:** It is this deeper spirit — this echo of worship from earlier Christmases — that we seek tonight as we hang the greens. We will welcome back some old friends: the Advent candles, evergreen garlands, Christmas tree, carols, and candles, as well as, certainly the familiar Bible stories and passages. Tonight we will introduce as new friends some white doves and white poinsettias to symbolize the true spirit of the season.

Over generations, Christians have associated the white dove with God's own Holy Spirit. It was by that Spirit that "the Word became flesh" and was born of the Virgin Mary. It was through the Spirit that our hope turned to realization and joy. Listen again to that story tonight.

**Scripture Reading:** Luke 1:26-38

**Congregational Praise Song:** "Father, I Adore You"
*(As the song is sung, the family enlisted to light the Advent candle comes forward.)*

**Lighting The Advent Candle Of Hope**


## II. The Spirit Of Life: Hanging The Evergreens

**Narrator:** The evergreen garlands and wreaths are "old friends" at Christmas. They bring life to our room, which calls to mind the life God gives us through the Savior, Jesus. With that life they bring beauty, fragrance, and joy, and that truly is what Jesus brings to us with his life when we invite him into our lives. As a reminder that life comes by the Spirit of God, we will add white doves to our garlands this year. Hear again the words of life now.

**Scripture Reading:** John 1:1-4 and Colossians 1:16-20

**Narrator:** Several families have volunteered to hang our evergreens at this time. As they work, we will hear a carol of worship.

**Solo:** "Let All Mortal Flesh Keep Silence"

**Hanging The Evergreens**


## III. The Spirit Of Peace: Adding White Poinsettias

**Narrator:** Another fresh touch this year is found in the delicate white poinsettia plants, which have been dressed for this occasion. White is the color of peace, the absence of conflict and challenge. We have chosen white this year to carry out our theme, "The Spirit Of Christmas." *(If individual families provided the plants, explain by whom and for whom the plants have been purchased, and thank the appropriate persons.)*

**Minister:** Just as Jesus is our life, and Jesus is our hope, so also Jesus is our peace. He made peace between God and us when we were far away and alienated. And he continues to make peace between factions of humankind trying to share this planet space. Hear again the words from the apostle Paul.

**Scripture Reading:** Ephesians 2:14-18 and Luke 2:14

**Congregational Carol:** "I Heard The Bells On Christmas Day"

**Placing The Poinsettias**
*(During the singing, ask the families who purchased plants, or another designated group, to bring them forward and place them at the appointed locations. If an offering is to be taken, ushers may be instructed to come forward on the final verse of the carol.)*

**Offering**

**Special Music:** "Lord, Make Me An Instrument Of Thy Peace"

### IV. The Spirit Of Sharing: Decorating The Tree

**Narrator:** One of the most individual of all our home decorations is our Christmas tree. Each family has a unique collection of ornaments. Some are specialized: all angels, all handmade, all Chrismons, all a certain color. Others are assortments: things the children have made through the years, things handed down from generations, gifts from friends.

**Minister:** It is this uniqueness that will make our tree very special this year. Families who wish to do so will share their personal ornaments for the tree. This means our tree will be gifted with a variety that reflects the rich diversity of our congregation; but which also shows the oneness we experience when we are together. We will call it a "Spirit of Sharing" tree. Let's think again of the prayer of Jesus for his church, and the admonition of Paul to the Ephesians.

**Scripture Reading:** John 17:20-23 and Ephesians 4:2-6

**Narrator:** If you have family ornaments to share, do that as we sing the next song. Others who wish to help may come and place the smaller white doves over the tree. Someone may climb the ladder and put the larger dove on the highest boughs. Then we will plug in the lights and enjoy our very unique "Spirit of Sharing Tree."

**Quiet Music:** "We Are One In The Bond Of Love"
*(as worshipers decorate the tree)*

**Decorating The Christmas Tree**

### V. The Spirit Of Celebration: Hanging The Banners

**Narrator:** Christmas remains one of the happiest seasons of the year. We celebrate many gifts all through the month: the gift of family and friends, the joy of giving, the fun of social gatherings. And we count our blessings as we look for those who have unusual needs and try to make their season happier, also. Joy and celebration are deeper for Christians than for others, because the spirit of the season is confirmed by the Spirit of God who lives within us. While others celebrate through the events and trappings, we celebrate with an inner joy that comes from Jesus himself.

**Minister:** Listen to these occasions of celebration from the familiar Bible stories.

**Scripture Readings:** (by the Minister or a series of Readers)
    Luke 1:46-49 — Mary, when she heard she would bear the Savior
    Luke 1:67-69 — Zechariah, when John the Baptist was born
    Luke 2:13-14 — the angels, announcing Jesus' birth
    Luke 2:20 — the shepherds, when they saw the baby
    Luke 2:28-32 — the old prophet, Simeon, when he held the baby

**Narrator:** As we join together in a wonderful carol of celebration, our banner bearers *(name the group selected to carry and hang the banners this year)* will bring our Christmas banners and hang them for us.

**Hanging The Christmas Banners**

**Congregational Carol:** "Joy To The World! The Lord Is Come"
*(During this carol, those who will bring the lighted votive candles should assemble quietly in the back of the worship room. Ask someone to be there with a lighted candle to light their votives as they get ready to bring them forward.)*

## VI. The Spirit Of Love: Reading The Christmas Story

**Narrator:** The room is almost ready, and it is time now to read the true story of Christmas from the Bible to our children. *(Invite all small children to join you on the platform. House lights are dimmed to about 30% of full.)* We have asked our middle school children *(or another group, such as grandparents)* to bring the lighted votive candles. If you would, please come now and stand on either side of the platform. We will read by your light.

**Minister:** As our candlelighters come, I will begin reading for you the greatest story of love ever told: the Christmas narrative from Luke. *(Reads by candlelight and dimmed room light.)*

**Scripture Reading:** Luke 2:1-20

**Congregational Carol:** "O Come, All Ye Faithful" (chorus only)
*(Candlelighters place candles in designated places, such as on the platform railings, as the congregation sings.)*

**Placing The Candles**

**Benediction Praise Song:** "Shine, Jesus, Shine" (chorus only)

# The Christmas Stranger

## A Multigenerational Drama For Christmas

**Bill Thomas**

# The Christmas Stranger

**Summary**

Jack Hanson is a wealthy business owner, husband, and father, in that order. He is consumed by work and making money. For reasons no one knows, he hates Christmas. His wife and children have no tangible needs, but they lack joy and a real relationship with Jack. They don't celebrate Christmas. Things change, though, when Jack hires a "happy go lucky" stranger to fix some things around the house. This "Christmas Stranger" brings joy and laughter to the Hanson home. Jack's wife and children begin to understand Christmas. Then, the four of them attempt an even greater challenge — to break through Jack's hard shell. That's when Jack remembers what it all means from "The Christmas Stranger."

**Characters**
- **Roy Marsh** — minister of the church in Oak Hills
- **Kate Marsh** — Roy's wife and director of the children's choir
- **Jack Hanson** — wealthy businessman in his late thirties to early forties
- **Sara James** — twelve-year-old who is Ashley Hanson's best friend
- **Tom Kingsman** — "handyman" who Jack hires to fix things around the house
- **Young Jack Hanson** — Jack as a ten-year-old (Scene 2)
- **Young Molly Hanson** — Jack's eight-year-old sister (Scene 2)
- **Grace Hanson** — Jack's mother
- **Robert Hanson** — Jack's father
- **Mrs. Firkins** — secretary at Hanson's Furniture
- **Mr. Wentworth** — wealthy businessman who deals with Jack
- **Annie Hanson** — Jack's wife
- **Taylor Hanson** — nine-year-old daughter of Jack and Annie
- **Ashley Hanson** — thirteen-year-old daughter of Jack and Annie
- **Miss Winifred Long** — older lady in town who has few friends
- **Maudie Bellamy** — town gossip who knows all the news and is eager to share
- **Claire Bellamy** — Maudie's sister, also a town gossip
- **Ed Crandle** — owner and operator of Crandle's General Store
- **Molly** — Jack's sister (Scene 11)

**Setting**

The story takes place in the town of Oak Hills in the early- to mid-1900s. Oak Hills is a typical small American town where everyone knows everyone else. The main industry in Oak Hills is Hanson Furniture, where some of the finest pieces of furniture are crafted. People from all over long for a Hanson piece of furniture.

- **Scene 1** — town square
- **Scene 2** — small wooden house in the plains of Kansas
- **Scene 3** — office of Hanson's Furniture Store

**Scene 4** — outside the Hanson home
**Scene 5** — living room of the Hanson home
**Scene 6** — in front of Miss Long's home
**Scene 7** — living room of the Hanson home
**Scene 8** — Crandle's General Store
**Scene 9** — living room of the Hanson home
**Scene 10** — street in Oak Hills
**Scene 11** — Oak Hills church

**Note:** If the stage can be divided into three sections, then stage left could be the office of Hanson Furniture, Crandle's General Store, and the street in Oak Hills; center stage could be the town square and the living room of the Hanson home; and stage right could be the small wooden house in Kansas, the outside of the Hanson home, and in front of Miss Long's house. Center stage can also serve as the church.

**Props**
    Christmas tree
    Christmas ornaments
    Christmas stockings
    Candy canes
    Empty bottle
    Table
    Plate of food
    Drinking glass
    Office furniture
    Briefcase
    Piece of paper (signifying a contract)
    Pen
    Purse
    Stryfoam balls (used as snowballs)
    Cane
    Chairs
    Mugs
    Couch
    Simulated fireplace
    Groceries
    Grocery bag
    Christmas decorations
    Plate of cookies
    Church furniture
    Bible
    Shelves
    Money — coins only

**Costumes**

Clothing should be appropriate for the early- to mid-1900s. Tom Kingsman wears overalls. Grace Hanson is dressed in tattered clothing, with a scarf in her hair and an apron on. Miss Winifred Long is a classy dresser and the Bellamy sisters are flamboyant in their dress.

**Running Time**

Approximately sixty minutes

---

## Scene 1

*(As the lights come up, people are in the town square of Oak Hills. A crowd is milling. Some are shopping and some are talking.)*

**Roy:** Kate, are we ready for the children's program tomorrow night?

**Kate:** I think we are. Our last practice is this afternoon.

**Roy:** Great. Oh look, there's Jack Hanson. I want to invite him to church tomorrow night.

**Kate:** *(frowns)* He's such a grump. I don't think he'll come.

**Roy:** *(smiles)* Come on, Kate. You never know what might happen. *(approaches Jack, who is fighting his way through the busy town square)* Good day, Jack. How are you?

**Jack:** Not good at all, pastor. Who is responsible for this mob? I can't even get to my office.

**Roy:** Relax, Jack. It's almost Christmas. Folks are getting some last minute shopping done and all sorts of things.

**Jack:** It's a waste of time in my book, preacher. Christmas is nothing.

**Roy:** *(smiles)* Jack, Jack, Jack. Grumpy on the outside, but soft and gooey on the inside *(pats Jack on the stomach)* just like a marshmallow toasted over a fire. See you later, Jack, and Merry Christmas!

**Jack:** Hmmph! I'll show him who's soft ... *(turns to leave, but runs into Sara)* Hey! Watch where you're going! Don't I know you?

**Sara:** Hi, Mr. Hanson. I'm Sara. You know, Ashley's friend.

**Jack:** Oh yes, well move aside, child. I have work to do.

**Sara:** I'm sorry, Mr. Hanson. I just wanted to give you this. *(hands Jack a candy cane)* Mrs. Marsh gave them to us. I thought you might like to have it. Merry Christmas.

**Jack:** *(stares at the candy cane, getting more upset and more angry; then grabs it and throws it to the ground)* I don't want it! Now, get away. I have to go! *(hurries off)*

*(Tom Kingsman has walked up behind Sara and observed this outburst. Sara turns to him, looking bewildered and sad.)*

**Sara:** What, what did I do wrong?

**Tom:** Sara, you didn't do anything wrong. Ol' Jack there just has some bad memories, that's all. You did just fine.

### Scene 2

*(The light comes up in a small, wooden house somewhere in the plains of Kansas. Two children are huddled by the window, eagerly looking out. A small, poorly decorated Christmas tree stands in the corner. There are no presents under the tree. Empty stockings hang on the mantle. As the lights come up, Christmas carolers can be heard singing. The children are fascinated and point as the songs continue.)*

**Young Jack:** Molly, look! Can you see them?

**Young Molly:** Yeah, Jack. Christmas makes me feel so wonderful. Do you think he'll come this time? He didn't last year.

**Young Jack:** I know, Molly. But he will this year, he's just gotta. Look! They're leaving.

**Both:** Bye! Bye! Thanks!

*(The children are waving good-bye to the carolers as their mother enters. She is dressed in tattered but clean clothes. Her hair is tied back with a scarf. She enters wearing an apron. In the apron pocket are two candy canes that no one can see, yet.)*

**Grace:** Wasn't that just marvelous children? *(walks over and puts her arms around her children at the window)*

**Young Jack:** Mom? You heard them, too?

**Young Molly:** I really love Christmas, don't you, Mom?

**Grace:** It is a very special time of year ...

**Young Molly:** *(looks at Grace and interrupts)* Do you think Santa will bring us any presents this year? He hasn't for a long time.

**Grace:** *(looks out the window, with a pained expression)* I hope so, dear. But you know that's not really what's important about Christmas, don't you?

**Young Jack:** We know, Mom. Christmas is about Jesus being born. That's why it's so special. God gave us a wonderful gift and that's why we give to others ...

**Young Molly:** *(interrupts)* And that's why Santa gives, too. I just know he'll come.

*(The three of them hug by the window. The moment of quiet reverence and love is broken by the loud crash of a door.)*

**Robert:** *(enters loudly and speaks loudly; has been drinking and enters carrying an empty bottle)* Well, Merry Christmas! And how is my family?

**Young Molly:** *(runs and hugs Robert)* Daddy, did you see them? They were here and I know he'll come, too. I just know it.

**Robert:** What are you talking about, child? I ain't seen nobody.

**Young Jack:** The Christmas carolers, Dad. That's what she means. Didn't you see them?

**Robert:** I ain't seen nobody ...

*(Jack walks over and pulls Molly away. They stand by the little tree. Grace approaches Robert who has clumsily sat at the table. She has a plate of food and a drink.)*

**Grace:** Robert, you must be hungry. Here, eat. I saved it for you.

*(She sets the plate down. Robert begins to eat and drink without looking up.)*

**Grace:** Uh, Robert, did you pick up the *(looks over to her children who are looking at the few tree ornaments)* presents?

**Robert:** *(suddenly looks up, clearly angry)* Presents? What presents? There ain't no presents this year and there ain't never gonna be any.

**Grace:** Robert, please. The children ...

**Robert:** *(cuts her off and goes to where the children are standing)* It's time you kids learned what this Christmas stuff really is. *(The children back away from the tree, frightened.)* It is nothing. That's it — nothing. There ain't no presents. There ain't no Santa Claus and there ain't no tree *(grabs the little tree and throws it to the floor; begins to leave, but stops at the door and pulls a few coins from his pocket)* Oh yeah. Here's the change ... see if you can buy any presents with that. *(leaves, throwing the coins on the floor)*

*(Grace stands dumbfounded. Molly is crying and Jack holds her, trying to comfort her.)*

**Grace:** *(walks over to her children and has them sit next to her on the floor)* Your daddy didn't mean that. Don't you believe it, not a word.

**Young Molly:** You mean Christmas is not nothing? What about gifts?

**Grace:** *(sighs and reluctantly pulls two candy canes from her pocket)* Well, look what I found. I guess Santa must have left these for you two here in my pocket. And don't forget, Christmas is really about Jesus, okay? I've got to clean up ...

*(Jack and Molly take the candy canes and stare at them. Grace gets up quickly and starts putting the house back together. Molly and Jack talk quietly.)*

**Young Molly:** Jackie, why is it like this? How come we never get a real Christmas? All we ever get are these stupid candy canes.

**Young Jack:** *(puts his arm around his little sister)* Don't cry, Molly. It won't always be like this ...

**Young Molly:** *(interrupts)* Yes it will, Jack. It was like this last year and the year before. I think Daddy's right. For us, Christmas is nothing. *(angrily throws her candy cane down and runs offstage)*

*(Young Jack is now alone on the stage. A single light illumines where he sits.)*

**Young Jack:** *(talks quietly to himself)* Molly's right. She's right. Christmas is nothing and I hate it. And I hate these stupid candy canes. *(breaks them in anger as the lights go to black)*

### Scene 3

*(It is now about 25 years later in the town of Oak Hills. Lights come up in the office of Hanson Furniture. Jack is sitting at his desk. He is obviously cold. His secretary, Mrs. Firkins, enters.)*

**Mrs. Firkins:** Mr. Hanson, a Mr. Wentworth is here to see you regarding an order for his stores. My, it sure is cold in here. The pipes aren't working yet?

**Jack:** Uh, no, Mrs. Firkins, they are not. Call for a handyman, will you? Thank you, Mrs. Firkins. Send in Mr. Wentworth. And do me a favor, will you? Close the curtains. That bunch on the square are irritating me.

**Mrs. Firkins:** Yes, sir. *(turns to leave, pauses at the window wondering how he could call the festivities "irritating"; closes the curtains and begins to leave, but pauses)* Oh, and sir, your wife sent a message that she will be stopping by soon. There is some problem at home.

**Jack:** Oh, very well. Thank you, Mrs. Firkins. Now, if you'll show Mr. Wentworth in.

*(Mrs. Firkins leaves and Jack resumes working at his desk waiting for Mr. Wentworth. Mr. Wentworth enters, carrying his briefcase.)*

**Jack:** Ah, Mr. Wentworth, good day to you. Have a seat, won't you? *(Mr. Wentworth sits)* It's a little chilly in here, but we'll soon have the heat back on. Can I get you anything?

**Mr. Wentworth:** *(takes contract from his briefcase)* Thank you, but no. Mr. Hanson, I've come today to finalize our contract. You'll see the total price we agreed upon at the bottom, for which you have agreed to provide tables, desks, and chairs to all my stores in the state, with the first shipment arriving in two weeks. Is everything in order?

**Jack:** *(smiles)* Oh, yes sir. We'll have the first shipment to you in two weeks. *(both sign the contract)* It has been a pleasure to do business with you.

**Mr. Wentworth:** *(stands)* It has been a pleasure working with you. *(turns to leave, but stops and speaks)* You know, Mr. Hanson, this deal will bring us both a lot of money, and that's good at Christmas, yes?

**Jack:** *(smiles again)* Oh yes. I've thought of that. Good day, Mr. Wentworth!

*(Mr. Wentworth leaves as Jack's wife, Annie, enters.)*

**Annie:** Jack, I'm sorry to bother you here, but we have a slight problem at home.

**Jack:** *(looks concerned)* We do? What is it?

**Annie:** Well, you know that swimming pool you've always wanted?

**Jack:** *(puzzled)* Yes?

**Annie:** We've got it.

**Jack:** We do?

**Annie:** We do — in the bathroom.

**Jack:** What? What happened?

**Annie:** The pipes burst and water was everywhere. *(starts to cry)* It looked like a fountain. It was just water, gushing everywhere ...

**Jack:** Okay. It will be fine. *(mutters)* I don't have time to fix it now with this new order. I'll just have to find someone else to do it. *(Tom Kingsman enters, whistling, with his hands in his pockets, just looking around)* Hey, buddy. What are you doing?

**Tom:** Nothin'. Just lookin' around.

**Jack:** What do you mean, "just looking around"? Who sent you? What is your business here?

**Tom:** Business? Oh yeah. I got business, all right.

**Jack:** Well?

**Tom:** Well what?

**Jack:** What's your business?

**Tom:** Oh, that. I fix things.

**Jack:** That's great. Just come right over here. These pipes haven't worked all day. Cold as ice in here. Get these fixed and see the lady ... Hey, I know. Are you *good* at fixing things?

**Tom:** *(smiles)* One of the best.

**Jack:** Good, good. *(pats Tom on the back)* When you finish, see my wife here for our address. I have some work for you to do there. *(to Annie)* See? Everything's gonna be just great. *(leaves)* Now, to make sure that order gets started....

*(Annie stands, looking after Jack. Tom stands off to the side, smiling.)*

**Annie:** Uh, Mr. Uh ...

**Tom:** Kingsman, ma'am. Tom Kingsman.

**Annie:** Mr. Kingsman, here is our address.

**Tom:** Annie, what can I do for you?

**Annie:** Do for me? Oh, you mean what's the problem? It's the plumbing. Something happened. There's water everywhere. It's a mess.

**Tom:** I'll be right over. Is there anything else?

**Annie:** *(hesitates)* No, I guess that's all. *(starts to leave)*

**Tom:** Okay! *(smiles)* See ya soon. Oh, hold on a minute. I've got something for ya.

*(Annie stops and Tom comes over to her.)*

**Tom:** *(hands Annie a candy cane)* Here. It's almost Christmas. These things, well I like 'em. They remind me of what it's all about.

**Annie:** Thank you. *(puts the candy cane in her purse)* See you later, then?

**Tom:** Sure thing, ma'am.

### Scene 4

*(The scene shifts to outside the home of Jack and Annie Hanson. It is supposed to be cold and snowy outside. Ashley and Taylor are outside playing. Tom Kingsman approaches.)*

**Tom:** *("forms" a styrofoam snowball and throws it at Taylor who is not looking)* Ha! Gotcha!

**Taylor:** No fair. I wasn't looking. Hey, who are you?

**Tom:** Oh yeah, I'm sorry. My name is Tom — Tom Kingsman. I'm here to fix some things in your house.

**Ashley:** It's about time. We still haven't got all the water out of the bathroom, yet. I'll go get Mother. *(leaves)*

**Tom:** So, Taylor, are you excited for Christmas?

**Taylor:** Nah. Daddy says, "Christmas is nothing" so we don't celebrate or anything. I don't really know very much about it.

**Tom:** *(looks incredulously)* You don't know about Christmas? Well, I'm glad we met, 'cause I know all there is to know about Christmas. I'm an expert on reindeer. Santa knows me by name. I know about important stuff, too — like Bethlehem and a manger. Just ask me and I'll tell you.

**Taylor:** Well, I've always wondered about angels. Are there really angels?

**Tom:** You bet there are. They are a big part of Christmas. Hey, have you ever seen one?

**Taylor:** No.

**Tom:** Well, I have, and it is grand. Do you want to make an angel, right here in the snow?

**Taylor:** I don't know how.

**Tom:** It's easy. I'll show you!

*(Tom and Taylor lay in the "snow" and make "snow angels." Tom pantomimes throwing snow on Taylor who does the same to Tom. They are laughing and giggling. Annie and Ashley enter. Annie is laughing, but Ashley looks grim and sober.)*

**Ashley:** What are you doing? Your clothes are soaked and you'll catch pneumonia. Mother, tell this, this Tom what you think.

**Annie:** *(smiles)* I think it is a wonderful snow angel, Taylor.

**Taylor:** Thank you, Mommy. Would you like to make one?

**Annie:** Uh, I don't ...

**Ashley:** *(interrupts)* Don't be ridiculous. Mother would never do that. That is the silliest thing I have ever heard ...

**Annie:** *(interrupts)* I don't think I'd mind at all. *(Ashley looks aghast, then turns and leaves as Annie begins to make a snow angel.)* Will you show me how, Tom?

**Tom:** Sure. It's like this. *(demonstrates and the three of them begin to flap their arms wildly in the snow, then rise)*

**Annie:** I don't know when I've ever had so much fun. Mr. Kingsman, thank you.

**Tom:** My pleasure, ma'am. *(Secretly, he and Taylor have styrofoam snowballs. They prepare to throw them at Annie, who notices them and they drop them.)* Well, I guess I'd better get to work. Mr. Hanson is going to want things fixed around here.

**Taylor:** Oh, Tom, do you have to go? I wanted to talk some more. I have a lot of questions about Christmas.

**Tom:** I'll tell you what, if it is okay with your mom, then you can help me. Is that okay, Mrs. Hanson?

**Annie:** I guess so, though I don't know how much help she'll be.

**Tom:** I think she'll do just fine. Taylor, what have you heard about Christmas?

**Taylor:** Well ...

*(Taylor and Tom exit, talking. Annie follows, smiling. Stage goes dark.)*

## Scene 5
*(The stage lights up with Tom and Taylor in the living room of the Hanson house.)*

**Tom:** Taylor, that job was harder than it looked. I didn't think we'd ever get that pipe fixed. Thanks for your help.

**Taylor:** Oh, Tom. You know I didn't do anything. Thank you for telling me about Christmas and Jesus. Thanks for this candy cane, too. *(pulls it out and puts it in her mouth)* I've never had one before. It is delicious!

**Ashley:** *(enters and notices the candy cane)* Hey! Where did you get that?

**Taylor:** None of your business. *(Ashley glares at her)* But, if you must know, Tom gave it to me. *(Tom turns and smiles at Ashley)*

**Ashley:** Mr. Kingsman, I do not think my father would want you to do that. We don't engage in such foolishness.

**Tom:** Ashley, I know what your father thinks, but what about you? What do you think of Christmas?

*(Jack and Annie enter just as Ashley is about to answer the question.)*

**Jack:** Hi, everyone. *(all stop talking; Taylor hides the candy cane behind her back)* What's going on?

**Taylor:** Oh, nothing Daddy. Tom and me fixed the pipes!

**Jack:** That would be Tom and I, dear.

**Taylor:** No, Daddy, it was Tom and me.

**Jack:** Taylor, I ...

**Annie:** *(interrupts)* You guys did a fantastic job! Tom is a great fixer! *(looks over at Tom, smiling)*

**Jack:** Yes, I suppose he is. Well, we must be going. Mr. Wentworth has generously offered to take us to dinner. It will be quite refreshing. Perhaps we can talk some more business. Come along, Annie. We shouldn't be late. *(leaves)*

**Annie:** *(sighs)* I look forward to a lovely evening. Good-bye.

**Tom:** Have a nice time and Merry Christmas!

**Jack:** *(stops and angrily turns to face Tom)* Mr. Kingsman, I would ask you to refrain from using those words around me or my family. We are quite content as we are. We do not need to celebrate such foolishness. You have no right to ...

**Annie:** *(interrupts and tugs on Jack's arm)* Jack, we should go. You don't want to be late.

**Jack:** *(calms down)* Yes, you're right. Let's go. Mr. Kingsman, I'll be watching you.

**Tom:** *(smiles)* I'll be watching you, too, Jack.

*(As Jack and Annie leave, Sara enters.)*

**Sara:** Hi, Ashley. I thought I'd come over. I know you don't normally do "Christmas stuff" and all but, well, I wondered if you wanted to go with some of us to Miss Long's house. We're gonna sing to her and see if she'll let us ride our sleds down her hill.

**Ashley:** Oh, Sara, I don't know. I have a lot of studying to do and ...

**Taylor:** *(interrupts)* Oh, Ashley, you can study anytime. Let's go. That is, if I can come, too?

**Sara:** Sure you can. More is better.

**Tom:** Good. Then I think I'll come, too. There's nothing I like better than to sing and go sledding with friends.

**Taylor:** Well, Ashley, what do you say? Will you come?

**Sara:** Yeah, Ashley, join in.

**Ashley:** Oh, all right. I'll do it.

## Scene 6
*(As the lights come up on stage, the children and Tom are in front of Miss Long's house. They will sing and pantomime sledding.)*

**Sara:** Hey, look! It's Pastor Marsh.

**Roy:** Hi, everyone. Kate and I are glad to see you. Sleds are ready, but first, the concert.

**Kate:** Is everyone ready? Sing out loud and strong, now. Let's make sure she hears us.

*(All loudly sing Christmas carols. Shortly thereafter, Miss Long appears.)*

**Miss Long:** *(enters, swinging her cane wildly)* What in blue blazes is going on here? Who are you and why are you here?

**Taylor:** Merry Christmas, Miss Long! We wanted to come by and sing to you, so you could have some, you know, Christmas cheer.

*(The children all nod in agreement and chime in with, "Yeah," "Right.")*

**Roy:** Miss Long, we figured you might like a little company so we decided to pay you a visit. We won't stay long ...

**Tom:** *(interrupts)* Merry Christmas, Winnie! *(hands Miss Long a candy cane)* Here have one. I've got plenty.

**Miss Long:** *(takes the candy cane and looks at it as the group prepares to leave)* Hey, wait a minute there, sonny. You just got here. What's that over there? Sleds, huh? You were hoping to use my hill to sled down.

**Kate:** Well, Miss Long. I can't lie to you. That was our hope.

**Miss Long:** Lie to me! Dearie, you'd better not lie to me. I've been known to cane a few whipper-snappers in my day! *(swings her cane wildly at them, then calms down)* Why yes, I can remember sledding. My papa would take us up to the very top of this hill. We called it "Terrifying Hill." We would climb on the toboggan, the three of us, and then he would push. We would go flying down the hill. *(pantomimes sledding, causing the children to laugh)* Whatcha' laughin' at, you youngsters? I can still do it, I bet.

**Taylor:** Will you, Miss Long?

**Miss Long:** Will I what?

**Tom:** You know, Winnie. Will you go sledding with us?

*(The children and Mr. and Mrs. Marsh encourage her, saying, "Yes," "Go," "Please.")*

**Miss Long:** Well, it has been a long time, but I think I still got it in these old bones. Come on, you urchins. Keep up and don't dawdle.

*(The group begins to march together around the stage. As they walk, the Bellamy sisters approach.)*

**Claire:** Maudie, do you see what I see? I can hardly believe my eyes! Is that old Winnie Long out there with those children? What in heaven's name does she think she's doing?

**Maudie:** Claire, if I hadn't seen her with my own eyes, I wouldn't have believed it. That old bat is gonna break her neck. Someone should tell her to act her age. It just ain't proper, I tell ya.

*(The group approaches the Bellamy sisters, with Miss Long in the lead.)*

**Miss Long:** Well, well, well. If it isn't the Tell-All twins. How are you, Claire and Maudie?

**Claire:** Why, we're just fine, Winnie. But I must say, we are a mite surprised by your choice of activity.

**Maudie:** What she means is, "What are you thinking of, woman?" You just can't go prancing around in the snow like that.

**Miss Long:** That's what I like about you, Maudie. You're so sensitive. You know, for a long time, I had forgotten what joy comes from Christmas.

**Claire:** Well, I never ...

**Miss Long:** *(interrupts)* And that's the problem, Claire. Now if you'll excuse us, we have a date with "Terrifying Hill."

*(Miss Long leads the group. As they pass by Maudie and Claire, Tom hands them both a candy cane and smiles. The scene closes with the Bellamys leaving on one side of the stage and the group leaving on the other side.)*

**Scene 7**
*(The lights come up on the living room in the Hanson house. Tom and Taylor are sitting by the fire, drinking hot chocolate, while Ashley is sitting on the couch.)*

**Taylor:** That was so much fun, Tom. Who would believe that ol' Miss Long could sled like that! She went flying over that bump. She must've been three feet in the air! *(pantomimes Miss Long flying through the air; while Ashley sits quietly, listening)*

**Tom:** *(laughing)* Well, you might say she was soaring with the angels.

**Taylor:** *(giggles)* Miss Long is really a nice lady. I don't think anyone has ever wished her a "Merry Christmas" before. She seemed to be surprised.

**Tom:** It has been a while, that's for sure. Miss Long remembers, though. She knows what it's all about.

**Taylor:** And thanks to you, Tom, I do, too.

**Ashley:** *(hesitantly)* Uh, Tom, Mr. Kingsman. I've been listening to you and Taylor and I watched Miss Long today. I've never seen her like that before. I know it has to be something about this Christmas thing, but I, well, I don't know what it is. Will you tell me?

**Tom:** Ashley, I would love to. Christmas is about love — God's love. He sent his Son, Jesus, so that people could go to heaven and be with him forever. It's like the old Christmas song, "Silent Night." Sing it with me, Taylor.

*(Tom and Taylor sing "Silent Night." At the conclusion, Tom gives Ashley a candy cane.)*

**Ashley:** Thank you. *(looks down at the candy cane in her hand)* I feel so foolish. Sara and all my friends were right. Tom, our family has missed so much.

**Annie:** *(enters and looks around, smiling)* Hey, what's going on here?

**Tom:** Oh, nothin' ...

**Ashley:** *(interrupts)* It's not nothing, Tom. It's not. Oh, Mom. *(runs to her mother and hugs her tightly)*

**Taylor:** *(looks at Tom)* Thanks for helping my sister. There's one more thing to fix, though ... *(pulls him down and whispers in his ear)*

## Scene 8

*(This scene opens in Crandle's General Store. It is Christmas Eve day. Jack is in the store, picking up a few items for dinner that evening.)*

**Mr. Crandle:** *(comes over to Jack)* How are you, Mr. Hanson? Can I get you anything?

**Jack:** Oh, no thanks, Ed. I think I'm finding everything I need. *(begins speaking to himself as Mr. Crandle returns to the counter)* Let's see, Annie wanted some sugar and flour — that's over there. Eggs — on the other side of the store. Vanilla flavoring? I don't even know what that is! What is she going to do with that?

*(As Jack is talking to himself and looking around the store, the Bellamy sisters enter.)*

**Maudie:** Wasn't that just splendid? I would have never believed that he could play like that!

**Claire:** I haven't sung and laughed like that in years. That Tom Kingsman, why he's an angel, he is.

*(Jack overhears the sisters talking and rolls his eyes and continues on a futile search for vanilla flavoring.)*

**Mr. Crandle:** Well, you ladies sure seem happy today, but after all, it's Christmas Eve, isn't it? What's the source of your joy on this fine afternoon?

**Claire:** Mr. Crandle, you just wouldn't believe it. You just wouldn't.

**Maudie:** That's right, Ed. It is downright unbelievable.

**Mr. Crandle:** What is? What happened?

**Claire:** Well, if you must know, Maudie and I have just finished practicing for the Christmas Eve service at church tonight.

**Maudie:** For the first time in thirty years ... *(Claire interrupts with an "ummh.")* I mean twenty years ... *(Claire interrupts again)*, I mean a long time, the Bellamy sisters will be singing!

**Mr. Crandle:** *(astonished)* You are? Well, that's just fantastic. It has been so long ...

**Claire:** *(interrupts)* Yes, since our papa died.

**Mr. Crandle:** Well, what happened?

**Maudie:** It was the strangest thing, really. Pastor Marsh sent a message for us to meet him at the church.

**Claire:** We thought he might want our ideas for Sunday's message.

**Maudie:** But when we got there, he wasn't there at all, but this young handyman fella was ...

**Claire:** His name is Tom Kingsman.

**Maudie:** I was getting to that. His name is Tom Kingsman ...

**Claire:** *(interrupts)* I said that.

**Mr. Crandle:** Uh, ladies, if you'll continue, please.

**Maudie:** Oh yes, of course. Sorry. Well, that Tom Kingsman was sitting at the piano when we came in and, oh, you should've heard what he was playing.

**Claire:** Straight from heaven, it was.

**Maudie:** It was just beautiful. When he saw us, he stopped. He asked us if we would like to join him. Well, I looked at Claire ...

**Claire:** *(interrupts)* And I looked at Maudie. We just had to join him.

**Maudie:** So we did, and oh my, it was glorious to sing once again.

**Claire:** Tom has a lovely voice, too, and when Brother Marsh walked in, well he asked us right there if we'd sing tonight.

**Mr. Crandle:** That's wonderful and a real blessing for the church, too. You know, that Tom Kingsman is a real good guy. He came in here this morning. He left me these. *(pulls out a box of candy canes)* He told me to give 'em out to any and everybody. Would you ladies like one?

*(Maudie and Claire take one and smile at one another. Jack finally emerges from behind the shelves. He has heard all, but pretends to be oblivious.)*

**Jack:** I found that vanilla stuff. Oh, Maudie, Claire, good afternoon. How are you doing?

**Maudie:** Just fine, thank you. *(holds her candy cane in her hand where he can see it)*

*(Jack quickly pays for his stuff. Mr. Crandle sacks it. The Bellamy sisters just look at Jack. It is an awkward moment.)*

**Mr. Crandle:** Thanks for coming in, Mr. Hanson. Merry Christmas! And oh, here, wait. Would you like one? *(offers a candy cane to Jack)*

**Jack:** *(stares at candy cane)* Uh, no. No thanks. *(quickly leaves the store)*

*(The lights dim.)*

### Scene 9
*(The lights come up on the living room of the Hanson home. Annie, Ashley, Taylor, and Tom are there. The room is different this time. There is a Christmas tree in the corner and stockings hung on the mantle. While Jack has been at the store, they have been decorating. Everyone is anxious for Jack to arrive.)*

**Annie:** *(hangs ornaments on the tree)* Hurry, girls! Your dad will be back soon. We want everything to look just right.

**Taylor:** Mom, do you think Dad will be mad at us for doing this? We've never done it before. *(hangs candy canes on the tree)*

**Annie:** I hope not, dear, but I'm sure it will surprise him. Ashley, have you found it?

**Ashley:** *(sitting on couch, looking at a Bible)* Yes, Mother. Here it is. I can't wait to read it to him.

**Annie:** Good. Now Tom, did you arrange for Mr. Crandle to pick her up? The telegram said she would arrive by 7:00 tonight.

**Tom:** Sure did.

**Ashley:** I just can't wait until Father comes ...

**Tom:** *(He has been helping with ornaments and also helped Ashley find the scripture. He smiles and hums a Christmas song.)* You won't have to wait, Ashley. I think I hear your father coming up the walk now.

**Annie:** *(nervous, but excited)* Okay, girls, quick. Let's get in our places. Taylor, grab that plate of cookies. Tom, you're over there by the tree. Ashley, bring the Bible.

*(All move quickly. Tom stands by the tree and the girls join their mother by the door. There is an anxious pause before Jack enters. Jack comes through the door, wearing his overcoat and hat.)*

**Ashley and Taylor:** Merry Christmas, Daddy!

*(Jack looks surprised, but not yet angry.)*

**Annie:** Oh, Jack *(hugs him, but he remains stiff)*, I know we don't usually do this, but this year, I don't know, it just seemed right.

*(Jack removes his hat, but he still has his coat on.)*

**Ashley:** Yeah, Dad. Tom explained to us about Christmas. Listen *(begins to read from the Bible)*, "And she gave birth to her firstborn son and wrapped him in swaddling clothes and laid him in a manger ..."

*(Jack stops her with a wave of his hand. He still hasn't said anything.)*

**Taylor:** Look, Daddy, Momma and me, oops, I mean, Momma and I baked Christmas cookies. Do you want one?

**Jack:** *(Stares at the cookies as Taylor offers him the plate. He picks up a cookie, but doesn't eat it. He stands and stares as his family looks at him, eagerly hoping that he'll join in. He speaks slowly, as if trying to control himself.)* Uh, if you'll excuse me. I need something from the kitchen. *(hurries away from the group)*

**Annie:** Wait, Jack. I'll go with you ...

**Jack:** *(quickly interrupts)* No! *(more calmly)* No, that's all right.

*(Annie, Ashley, and Taylor look sad.)*

**Tom:** *(to the ladies)* You stay here. I'll check on Jack. *(moves over to where Jack stands)*

**Jack:** *(angrily)* What do you want?

**Tom:** I just want to help, Jack. What is it?

**Jack:** You've caused nothing but trouble since you've been here. Stirring up my family and getting them to do foolish things. You've got the whole town acting loopy. You're, you're ...

**Tom:** I'm what, Jack?

**Jack:** You're crazy, that's what.

**Tom:** Not exactly, Jack, but good try.

**Jack:** What are you talking about?

**Tom:** I know, Jack. I know.

**Jack:** You know what? *(his anger is rising)*

**Tom:** I know about you and Molly. I know about the little tree. I know about your father ...

**Jack:** *(interrupts angrily)* What? You don't know anything!

**Tom:** And I know about the candy canes and about ...

**Jack:** *(Angrily cuts him off and storms back into the room with the ladies. Tom follows. As Jack speaks, his anger grows.)* You don't know nothin'. And this Christmas foolishness *(goes over to the decorated tree, grabs it, and throws it to the floor)*, it is nothin', I tell you. Nothin'! *(storms out of the room, leaving Annie, Taylor, and Ashley dumbstruck)*

*(Tom goes over to Annie. The girls are huddled by their mother.)*

**Tom:** It will be all right, Annie. Let's get this tree back up.

**Annie:** Yes, yes. Let's do. Hurry, girls. We don't want to be late for church tonight.

*(The stage darkens as they begin to pick up what Jack has destroyed.)*


## Scene 10
*(Jack is alone, walking the streets of Oak Hills. He is huffing and puffing because he has been running.)*

**Jack:** Can you believe the nerve of that guy! I don't know what he's up to, but I will find out. Snooping around in our business. How can he know those things? He's been up to no good, that's for sure. What I can't figure out, though, is why Annie is acting so foolishly, and the children and the whole town! Has everyone gone nuts? *(continues to pace back and forth nervously)* I've got to do something. *(stops as he notices a bright star in the sky)* What in heaven's name is that? I've never seen a star so bright. *(Jack is drawn to follow the brightness of the star. As he does, he gets closer to the church. He hears singing. From offstage, voices are singing "Joy To The World.")* What's that song? It sounds familiar to me.

*(Jack wanders in the direction of the church. The stage goes to black.)*

## Scene 11

*(The final scene of the play takes place inside the church in Oak Hills. The whole town is there. They are standing and singing as Jack enters unobtrusively from the back. The congregation finishes. Pastor Marsh is at the front of the church directing.)*

**Roy:** That was wonderful. And now to read the Christmas story from the gospel of Luke is Ashley Hanson.

*(Ashley walks up to the front. Her friend, Sara, pats her on the back.)*

**Ashley:** Until a few days ago, I didn't have any idea what this Christmas thing was all about. But thanks to my sister and my best friend, Sara, and, of course, Tom, now I know. Here it is. *(begins to read the Bible)* "And she brought forth her firstborn son and wrapped him in swaddling clothes and laid him in a manger because there was no room for them in the inn. Now there were in the same country, shepherds abiding in the fields keeping watch over their flocks by night. And lo, the Angel of the Lord came upon them and the glory of the Lord shone round about them and they were sore afraid. But the angel said to them, 'Fear not! For behold I bring you good tidings of great joy which shall be to all people. For unto you is born this day, in the city of David, a Savior, who is Christ the Lord.'"

**Roy:** Beautiful, Ashley. Now, before I share with you tonight, a young lady has asked to say a few words. Let's give a warm welcome to Taylor Hanson.

*(The congregation applauds warmly. Tom, who is sitting beside Taylor, pats her on the back for encouragement.)*

**Taylor:** *(stands up front, nervously)* Thank you, Pastor Marsh. Like Ashley said earlier, we didn't know anything about Christmas until a few days ago. But, I want to thank my friend, Tom. He helped me see what it really means. He taught me about the shepherds, the angels, and the Baby Jesus, and God's love. That's what really matters.

**Miss Long:** You tell them, child.

**Taylor:** *(emotions rising)* This is the best Christmas I've ever had. It would be perfect if ... *(her voice breaks)* if only my daddy could see it. I know a lot of you think my daddy is mean and angry. But he's not really. He just hasn't seen the miracle of what it's all about.

**Jack:** *(He has been sitting in the back listening. He now stands and speaks. The congregation is surprised to see him. He walks up to where Taylor stands.)* I haven't seen it, but it's because I haven't wanted to. I had so much anger in me that I couldn't stand the thought of something good and special, like Christmas. All I knew about this time of year was hate and disappointment. But listening to you all here *(Tom, Annie, and Ashley have joined them up front)* I see now that there is love — God's love, and the love of family and friends.

**Taylor:** *(takes a candy cane from Tom)* Daddy, this is for you. It's more than candy, you know. The shape is a "J" for Jesus. The white shows us that we can be white as snow and the red reminds us of his blood. You see, Daddy, this candy cane represents the greatest gift of all.

*(Jack takes the candy cane and smiles. Everyone claps and comes forward to congratulate Jack. Then there is a rustling down the center aisle. Mr. Crandle is coming in carrying bags. He is followed by a well-dressed lady.)*

**Kate:** Oh, Mr. Crandle, you're here. And who is that with you?

*(Before Mr. Crandle can speak, Jack has broken through the crowd. He comes to the lady and they hug.)*

**Jack:** Molly! Is that you? Oh, Molly! *(hugs her)* Everyone, this is my sister, Molly, from New York. How did you get here?

**Molly:** Annie wired me and told me this was going to be a special Christmas. Told me I shouldn't miss it. I came right away. Mr. Crandle here picked me up at the train station. Well, Jackie, is this one special?

**Jack:** You bet it is, Molly. It sure is. *(He hands her a candy cane. They smile at one another. Then Jack mouths a "thank you" to Tom who is leaving out of the back of the church.)*

*(The entire cast then leaves the stage, handing out candy canes to all in the audience.)*

The End

# The Christmas Stranger Returns

## A Multigenerational Drama For Christmas

## Bill Thomas

# The Christmas Stranger Returns

**Summary**

Jack and Annie Hanson are leading citizens of the town of Oak Hills. Jack owns the furniture factory in town and is a wealthy man. A few years ago, Jack had an encounter with a Christmas Stranger that changed the way he viewed Christmas. Jack is now a Christian. He and his wife try to model their faith. One of the "big" events of the year is the annual Christmas Eve party at their home. Jack is very content with his life, and he has everything a man could want. This Christmas Eve, however, Jack's secure world is shaken. Someone from his past reappears just as a tragedy strikes. Jack is on the edge of losing it when the Christmas Stranger returns.

**Characters**

    **Narrator** — speaks as a person of the town
    **Eldon Kraft** — Jack's new factory manager and friend
    **Annie Hanson** — Jack's wife and a woman who is up to the challenge of Jack's bluster
    **Jack Hanson** — owner of Hanson Furniture and leading citizen of Oak Hills
    **Bobby Kraft** — Eldon and Martha's oldest son
    **Ashley Hanson** — Jack and Annie's oldest daughter
    **Toby Kraft** — Eldon and Martha's youngest son and Taylor Hanson's nemesis
    **Taylor Hanson** — Jack and Annie's youngest daughter
    **Ellen Kraft** — Eldon and Martha's oldest child
    **Martha Kraft** — Eldon's wife and Annie's best friend
    **Grace Hanson** — Jack's mother
    **Robert Hanson** — Jack's father
    **Tom Kingsman** — "handyman" and the "Christmas Stranger"
    **Bertram Gorsch** — owner of Gorsch Funeral Chapel in Oak Hills and the interest of the Bellamy sisters
    **Claire Bellamy** — one of the Bellamy sisters who have become legend in Oak Hills
    **Maudie Bellamy** — the other Bellamy sister
    **Sara James** — Ashley Hanson's best friend
    **Dr. Leland** — the town doctor
    **Milton Olson** — the minister of Oak Hills church
    **Mrs. Firkins** — Jack Hanson's secretary

**Setting**

The play takes place in the small Midwestern town of Oak Hills in the mid-1900s.

**Set**

    The stage can be divided into three parts:
        Stage right is the town
        Center stage is the Hanson home
        Stage left is the train for Scene 2 and Taylor's bedroom from Scene 3 to the play's end

**Props**
- Living room furniture
- Couch pillow
- Simulated fireplace
- Cupcakes
- Punch bowl
- Pictures in a long roll
- Candy canes
- Grocery list
- Mop
- Dust rag
- Bed
- Chairs
- Christmas tree
- Punch and cookies
- Hat

**Costumes**

The characters are dressed in conservative mid-1900s clothing. Jack and Annie are fairly wealthy, so their dress is more expensive looking. Maudie and Claire dress flamboyantly.

**Running Time**

Approximately sixty minutes

---

## Scene 1

*(The lights come up on the Narrator as he stands in front of the Hanson's living room. When he finishes his opening remarks, the lights come up on the living room.)*

**Narrator:** Good evening and welcome back to the town of Oak Hills. Much has changed since we were here last; especially Jack's attitude toward Christmas. Jack and his family are living the Christian faith and Jack, especially, is determined to never let Christmas pass without delving into what it all means. On this night, just a day before Christmas Eve, Jack has invited his good friend, Eldon Kraft, and his family to enjoy the evening. I believe dinner is just now finished. Listen, I think I hear them coming....

*(Jack and Eldon lead the way into the living room. They are followed by Taylor, Toby, Ashley, Bobby, Annie, Martha, and Ellen.)*

**Eldon:** My, Jack *(pats his stomach)*, that sure was a fine meal. Annie, you sure know your way around the kitchen.

**Annie:** Thank you, Eldon. You are very kind.

**Jack:** *(smiles)* Yes, Eldon, too kind. I guess Annie does have a few good qualities. *(looks at Annie)* I think I'll keep her around for a while.

*(Annie tosses a pillow from the couch at Jack. She, Jack, and the Krafts are all laughing.)*

**Bobby:** *(speaks to Ashley)* Uh, Ashley, I was wondering if ... uh ...

**Ashley:** *(doesn't hear Bobby's stammering, and announces to the group)* Hey, I'd like some punch. Anyone else want some?

**Toby:** I would! I would! Hey, do you have any of those cupcakes left? They were great.

**Taylor:** Oh brother! You've already had five. How many can you eat, you oinker?

*(Ashley, Toby, and Taylor go to the side of the living room where the punch bowl is. Bobby speaks to himself and Ellen overhears.)*

**Bobby:** Ugh! Why can't I ever talk to her?

**Ellen:** Why don't you try using the English language? That may help.

**Toby:** *(speaks to Ashley and Taylor)* Hey, what are you doing Christmas day? We're leaving that morning for my grandma's house.

**Ashley:** We usually stay here and have a big dinner.

**Taylor:** I wish we could go to Grandma's. Nana, Mom's mom, has lived by herself since Papa died. She doesn't cook or have big parties.

**Toby:** What about your dad's folks?

**Taylor:** I don't remember seeing them. I wish I could, though.

*(Their parents, who are sitting on the couch, now speak so the audience can hear.)*

**Jack:** Well, Eldon, if you'd like, I can show you the reports of that sales meeting ...

**Annie:** *(interrupts)* Oh, Jack, not now, it's almost Christmas. Do you have to think about work?

**Jack:** No. You're right, dear. Eldon, we'll check that out later.

**Martha:** Annie, I know. Let's all go to the parlor where we can show the fellas that new dance for the Christmas program.

**Annie:** Now that sounds like fun. Hey, kids, come on.

**Jack:** Do we have to go?

**Eldon:** Come on, Jack. Loosen up a little. Hurry up, kids!

*(Martha and Annie excitedly leave first. Eldon pulls Jack along. Ellen walks off, laughing at her brothers. Bobby awkwardly tries to say good-bye to Ashley. She doesn't hear him and walks off with Ellen. Bobby then leaves by himself. Toby and Taylor remain.)*

**Toby:** *(holds a cupcake in his right hand as he taps Taylor on the back with his left)* Oh, Taylor?

*(She turns disgustedly as he taps her shoulder. She then turns the other way right into a cupcake! Toby laughs and runs off.)*

**Taylor:** Toby Kraft! You dumb ape! I'll get you.... *(runs after Toby)*

*(The lights dim.)*

### Scene 2

**Narrator:** Oh, the joys of family life! While the Hansons and the Krafts have been enjoying a lovely evening, a train is only a few miles from the Oak Hills station. It is almost Christmas Eve. A young man aboard the train is attempting to lighten the day of the weary travelers.

*(The lights come up as the scene opens aboard the train as Tom Kingsman leads the travelers in a medley of lively Christmas songs.)*

**Grace:** Oh, Robert, wasn't that wonderful?

**Robert:** *(hasn't joined in the singing; just stares out of the window)* Oh, uh, yeah. It was fine.

**Grace:** Robert, you're not worried, are you?

**Robert:** What, me worried? Well, a little. It has been so long, Grace. What if...?

**Grace:** Don't you worry. I've written Annie several times. They'll be glad to see us.

**Robert:** I know you've written to Annie, but what about Jack?

**Grace:** Robert, we've been praying about this and I know it is the right time. We just have to trust, that's all.

*(Tom Kingsman approaches as Grace places her hand on Robert's hand.)*

**Tom:** Oh, I'm sorry. I didn't mean to interrupt ...

**Grace:** You didn't. That sure was some fine singing.

**Tom:** Well, thank you. I love Christmas. Where are you folks off to?

**Grace:** We are going to my son's house. It's been a long time since we've seen them. My grandchildren have grown too much.

**Tom:** You have grandchildren?

**Grace:** I sure do. Here are some pictures. *(pulls out a long roll of pictures)* This is Ashley. Isn't she a lovely young lady? She is fourteen now. Soon the boys will come around. And this is Taylor. Isn't she a baby doll? She is nearly twelve! Can you believe it?

**Tom:** It is a lovely family. They look familiar to me.... *(to Robert)* You must be so proud.

**Robert:** Uh, well, yeah. Sure I am. Listen, we don't want to keep you from what you're doing ...

**Tom:** Okay. But if you need anything, you just let me know.

**Robert:** Uh, sure, maybe. I don't know.

*(Tom moves on to lead some more Christmas singing. Grace reaches out to hold Robert's hand. The scene closes as the carols resume on the train.)*

### Scene 3

*(The lights come up on the town square as people are wandering around.)*

**Narrator:** It isn't easy trying to make things right again. It's also not easy getting ready for Christmas Eve, at least not for the Hanson family.

**Annie:** All right, everyone. I have to meet Martha here so we can get the decorations for tonight's party. Jack, I need you to take this list to Crandle's and don't forget that extra jug of milk.

**Jack:** I know, Annie, I know. I won't forget. *(As he answers, his mind is already wandering. He is brought back by the sight of the Krafts coming into the square.)* Eldon! Eldon, my friend. How are you? Boy, am I glad to see you.

**Eldon:** Why, Jack? Has Annie got a list of things for you to do that you want to get out of?

**Jack:** Of course, why else would I be so happy to see you? *(While Jack and Eldon are speaking to one another, Bertram Gorsch, the town's undertaker, approaches.)* Oh no, look, it's that creepy Gorsch fellow.

**Eldon:** I agree on that, Jack. He's a strange one.

**Annie:** Oh, you two! He's just different, that's all.

**Martha:** I understand that he's quite the ladies' man, too, especially with the Bellamy sisters! *(all laugh)*

**Annie:** Merry Christmas, Mr. Gorsch!

**Jack:** Yeah, Merry Christmas, Bert! How's business?

**Bertram:** That's Bertram, and business is simply wonderful. People here are just *dying* to see me. *(laughs obnoxiously at his own joke; Jack, Eldon, Martha, and Annie just look at each other and roll their eyes)*

**Eldon:** Well, Bert, I mean, Mr. Gorsch, do you have any special plans for Christmas?

**Bertram:** Why, of course, dear boy. This afternoon, when the bell tolls.... *(stops)* Oh my, I've told another one, haven't I? *(laughs obnoxiously and again the group looks away)* Anyway, when the bell tolls three, I will be dining with two of the leading citizens of this fair community. I'm sure you know them. Oh, I think I hear them now ...

*(The Bellamy sisters enter and come in dressed to the hilt. Claire has a new hat. Maudie is sporting a new dress. They are passing out candy canes to everyone they meet and wishing them a Merry Christmas. Both enter with a flourish. They see Bertram and make a mad dash for him, ignoring the rest.)*

**Claire:** Oh, Bertram, how simply divine it is to see you here on such a fine morning. I have so longed to show you my new chapeau.

**Maudie:** What she means, Bert old boy, is she wants to show you her new hat.

**Claire:** *(glares at Maudie)* Bertram, don't pay any attention to her. *(takes Bertram's arm and speaks to him away from the others)* I hope you like it, the hat, that is.

**Bertram:** Why yes, my dear. It is as lovely as you are.

**Claire:** *(blushes)* Oh, Bertram ...

**Maudie:** Oh brother! Bert, Claire wants you to know that she and I will be singing tonight at the Hanson party. She would like it a lot if you'd come. *(Claire is obviously embarrassed at her sister's boldness)*

**Bertram:** *(claps)* That will be marvelous, ladies. Furthermore, I can't wait until we meet for lunch this afternoon. Until then, duty calls. *(bows and leaves with a flourish; Claire is mesmerized; Maudie is nonplused by him)*

**Claire:** Good day and Merry Christmas! Oh my, Maudie, look what we have here. It's the Hansons and the Krafts. What good fortune.

**Maudie:** Oh, my goodness, yes, Claire dear. Annie, we were going to stop by your place, but, well, here you are. We have something to tell you. I know it will just make you burst with joy.

**Annie:** *(pauses awkwardly before she answers)* Well ...

**Maudie:** Well what?

**Claire:** Oh, for heaven's sake. Tell her the news.

**Maudie:** Oh, right. My goodness. I almost forgot. We will be at your house tonight and, as you heard, we will sing!

**Annie:** That's wonderful, ladies. *(Jack rolls his eyes and looks to Eldon.)* Be sure to arrive just after the church service.

**Maudie:** Oh, and that's not all. We'll be bringing our family's Christmas treat.

**Claire:** It's a recipe passed down from generations of Bellamys. We're bringing ...

**Maudie:** *(interrupts)* We're bringing our spinach and eggplant holiday rolls. *(The Hansons and Krafts share a look of panic.)* It will be great. I'll save a special one for you, Jack Hanson.

**Jack:** Oh, that's great, Maudie. I'm sure I will ... *(Annie elbows him)* I'm sure I'll love it.

**Claire:** Well, fine then. We must be on our way. *(to no one in particular)* That Bertram is such a honey. I know he loves this new hat. What do you think, Maudie dear?

**Maudie:** I told you before, Claire. It looks like a chicken built a nest on your head!

**Claire:** Why, of all the nerve, and you wearing that dress that looks like it was made from one of Crandle's feed sacks! *(The Bellamy sisters exit, arguing with one another.)*

**Martha:** Those two are something.

**Jack:** I'll say. They are a pair of ...

**Annie:** *(interrupts)* They're a pair of dear, sweet ladies. Martha, let's get moving. We've got to get to the bakery before all the good stuff is gone. Come with us, Ellen. Jack, don't forget my list.

**Jack:** *(holds up the list)* Don't worry, dear. I've got it. *(turns to Eldon)*

**Bobby:** Hey, all the gang is going to Terrifying Hill this morning. It's gonna be the greatest sledding day ever. We've got to go.

**Ashley:** I know, but we're stuck here.

**Bobby:** I'd ask if we can go, but Dad usually says, "No."

**Ashley:** I'd ask, too, but, I don't think my dad would let us, either.

**Toby:** Hey, Taylor, you ask him. He never tells you, "No."

**Taylor:** Oh, all right. Somebody's got to do it. *(to Jack)* Daddy?

**Jack:** *(stops talking to Eldon)* What, Taylor?

**Taylor:** Well, a bunch of kids are going to Terrifying Hill to sled today. I was wondering, well, can we go, too?

**Jack:** I don't know. We've got so much to do ...

**Ashley and Taylor:** *(interrupts)* Please, Dad. *(Toby and Bobby are looking hopefully to Eldon)*

**Jack:** Well, okay, but don't be late. Your mom'll be mad at me if you're not home on time.

**Bobby:** Does that go for us, too, Dad?

**Eldon:** Sure, just be careful.

**Bobby, Toby, Ashley, and Taylor:** Yahoo! Last one there pulls the sled up.

**Jack:** *(to Eldon)* Hey, great. They're all gone. Let's take a look at the gun shop. I saw this new ...

**Eldon:** *(interrupts)* But what about Annie's list?

**Jack:** We'll get it later. *(crumples the list and stuffs it in his pocket)*

*(The lights dim.)*

## Scene 4
*(This scene takes place in the living room of the Hanson house.)*

**Narrator:** Jack and Annie have returned home from town. Everything is nearly ready for the Christmas Eve party tonight. Little does Jack know that an unexpected visitor is about to change his life.

**Annie:** Jack, after you finish dusting, you'll need to make sure that we have enough firewood to last the evening.

**Jack:** Gee, Annie, I seem to be the only one working around here. Let's make the girls do something.

**Annie:** Well, we could have, but you told them they could go sledding.

**Jack:** I know, I know *(under his breath but still audible to Annie)*, I wish I had gone with them.

**Annie:** What did you say, Jack?

**Jack:** Nothing, dear.

*(There is a knock at the door.)*

**Jack:** I'll get it, Annie. Don't trouble yourself, dear. *(opens the door)*

**Ellen:** *(enters)* Good afternoon, Mr. Hanson. Is Mrs. Hanson home? I was hoping to practice my song for tonight.

**Jack:** Come on in, Ellen. I'm sure Annie ...

**Annie:** *(interrupts)* Hi, Ellen! I'm glad you came by. I'd love to go over that song with you. Let me put this mop away and I'll be right back. *(exits and puts the mop away)*

**Jack:** You two go right ahead and sing. I'm sure it won't bother me ...

**Annie:** *(reenters and interrupts)* Hush, Jack. *(to Ellen)* Don't pay any attention to old Scrooge there. Let's do your lovely song.

*(Ellen and Annie practice a Christmas song while Jack continues to dust and mutter to himself.)*

**Ellen:** Thank you, Mrs. Hanson. I'm just so nervous when I sing.

**Annie:** Don't be. You are singing to the Lord. It will be just fine. You'll see.

**Ellen:** Thank you, Mrs. Hanson. I guess I'd better go, Mom's expecting me. I'll see you tonight.

**Jack:** Oh yeah, bye, Ellen.

*(Ellen leaves.)*

**Annie:** Jack, why couldn't you have been more supportive?

**Jack:** Hey, I thought I was. Maybe if ... *(interrupted by a knock at the door)*

**Annie:** *(answers the door and is surprised)* Mom and Dad? Is that you? Come in, come in.

*(Robert and Grace enter, Grace hugs Annie.)*

**Grace:** Hello, Annie, Jack. We just arrived by train. I hope we didn't come at a bad time.

**Annie:** No, of course not. Come, sit here.

*(Grace sits next to Annie. Jack sits in the chair and Robert reluctantly sits next to Grace.)*

**Grace:** Hello, Jack.

**Jack:** Mom, it's good to see you. *(looks to Robert, but says nothing)*

**Annie:** Tell us about your trip. I got your wire, but didn't know when to expect you. Grace, why don't you help me in the kitchen? I have some punch here and some cookies ...

**Jack:** *(interrupts)* I'll help you, Annie. *(stands to leave)*

**Annie:** No, your mom can come. *(takes Grace by the arm, and they exit, leaving Jack and Robert alone)*

**Robert:** *(awkwardly)* So, you've got a nice place here.

**Jack:** Yeah, thanks.

**Robert:** You're doing well, I see.

**Jack:** I'm doing fine.

**Robert:** Uh, look, son ...

**Jack:** *(interrupts)* Hold it! Stop right there! Don't call me that.

**Robert:** But I ...

**Jack:** *(interrupts again)* You weren't there for us. You never cared for us. You have never been a dad to Molly or me.

**Robert:** I know, Jack. You're right. I deserve that, every bit of it. I want you to know, though, that I'm sorry. I'm not the same now as I used to be ...

**Jack:** *(interrupts again)* It's too late ...

**Annie:** *(interrupts Jack as she and Grace enter)* Here, fellows, enjoy. *(hands out punch and cookies, then there is an awkward pause)*

**Jack:** *(breaks the silence)* Well, I have to go into town. I forgot something on your list.

**Grace:** Robert, why don't you go, too?

**Robert:** Uh, well, I don't ... *(a knocking at the door interrupts him)*

**Jack:** Who could that be? *(opens the door to a frantic Sara)*

**Sara:** Mr. Hanson, Mr. Hanson! There's been an accident. It's Taylor. She's hurt!

**Annie:** Oh no, Jack!

**Jack:** Stay here. I'll go and get her.

**Robert:** I'm going, too. You may need the help.

## Scene 5

*(This scene takes place in the Hanson home. Taylor is in the bedroom, stage left. Jack is standing by Taylor's bed with Annie. Dr. Leland is with them.)*

**Narrator:** Jack and Robert arrived as Crandle did with Dr. Leland. Taylor was unconscious when she was brought home and has stayed that way. It is not the Christmas Eve that everyone expected.

**Jack:** How is she, doc?

**Dr. Leland:** Jack, Annie, I've checked her over thoroughly. She's cracked a rib and broken her wrist. There doesn't appear to be any internal bleeding. We need for her to regain consciousness. I've contacted the hospital in Bridgetown. We now must wait and pray.

**Annie:** *(hugs Jack, cries softly)* Oh, Jack, what are we going to do?

**Jack:** You heard the doc, Annie. We pray.

**Dr. Leland:** Let me stay with her for a while. Pastor Olson is on his way. You two get some rest.

*(Jack and Annie enter the living room. Ashley is sitting there next to Bobby and crying. The Krafts are there with Jack's parents. Toby is quiet in the corner. Martha talks to Grace while Eldon and Robert talk to each other.)*

**Ashley:** *(cries)* It's my fault. I shouldn't have let her ...

**Bobby:** *(interrupts)* No, Ashley. It's not your fault. It's nobody's fault.

**Ashley:** Oh, Bobby. *(buries her head in Bobby's shoulder; he is reluctant, but decides to hold her while she cries)*

**Eldon:** *(to Jack)* How are you doing?

**Jack:** I'm okay. We just wait, that's all. And pray.

**Eldon:** I will, my friend, I will.

*(There is a knock at the door. Pastor Olson enters.)*

**Pastor Olson:** I'm so sorry, Jack, Annie. How is she?

**Annie:** *(goes over to Grace and Martha)* The doctor says she's got some injuries but the big thing is that she needs to wake up. I don't know ... *(breaks into tears)*

**Martha:** Oh, Annie. It will be all right. You'll see.

**Grace:** That's right, dear. Just trust and pray.

**Jack:** I can't just sit here and wait. I've got to go!

**Annie:** Oh, Jack, where?

**Jack:** *(shouts as he leaves)* Anywhere!

**Eldon:** I'll go with him.

**Robert:** No, you stay. Let me go.

*(Eldon returns to the group as Robert leaves. He and Pastor Olson and the ladies form a prayer circle. The lights go out.)*

## Scene 6

*(The scene opens in the town square of Oak Hills. It is deserted on this Christmas Eve, or so it appears.)*

**Narrator:** It's cold on the town square tonight. Christmas Eve; most folks are enjoying the night with family and friends. It is a night of joy, happiness, and expectation. Jack, though, finds himself alone with his doubts and fears. He is used to controlling things, but he can't control this.

**Jack:** *(speaks as if to God in heaven)* Why, God, why? What have I done? I've changed, don't you remember? I'm doing what you want me to do. Don't take my daughter. Please, God, I don't understand.

**Robert:** *(approaches Jack in the dark square)* Sometimes we don't, son.

**Jack:** What are you doing here?

**Robert:** Don't you see, Jack? We are doing the same thing. You're here trying to save your daughter and I'm here trying to save my son.

**Jack:** But ...

**Robert:** *(interrupts)* Listen, Jack. I know I can't make up for what I've done. I understand if you don't want me as your father and I don't blame you. But I, well, I'm gonna be here for Taylor. I'll stand with you, Jack. No matter what.

*(Jack looks to Robert in an uncertain way. The moment is interrupted by the singing of Tom Kingsman.)*

**Tom:** *(enters singing "Joy To The World")* Oh, I'm sorry. I didn't mean to interrupt.

**Jack and Robert:** Hey, it's you. What are you doing here?

**Robert:** Do you know this fellow?

**Jack:** Sure, I met him a few years ago. You?

**Robert:** I just met him on the train out here.

**Tom:** You both know me and I know you. I also know why you're here. *(continues to hum the song)*

**Jack:** If you know, then how can you be singing? It's Taylor! You remember her. She's hurt bad. Come, I'll show you.

**Tom:** I can't, Jack.

**Jack:** What do you mean, you can't?

**Tom:** It's not my assignment.

**Jack:** Not your assignment? What do you mean? What am I supposed to do?

**Tom:** Pray, Jack. Tell God what's in your heart.

**Jack:** Why is God allowing this, Tom? Why would he take my baby?

**Tom:** I don't know, Jack. But he does know how you feel. It was on a night like this that he gave his Son to the world, remember? He knows. I'll see you later, Jack. You, too, Robert.

**Robert:** Come on, son. Let's go home.

*(The lights dim.)*

## Scene 7

*(This scene takes place in the living room of the Hanson home. The mood is far from the festive party that should have been. The Bellamy sisters are standing and talking with Grace. Bertram Gorsch is with them. Mr. Crandle and Mrs. Firkins are in the back of the living room. Martha and Ellen are sitting next to Annie, who is on the couch. Ashley is near the bedroom. Bobby stands next to her. Eldon is by the window, talking to Pastor Olson. Toby is by himself, near the Christmas tree.)*

**Narrator:** Not what was expected here tonight, I'm afraid. But then, the unexpected almost always occurs on Christmas Eve.

**Toby:** *(comes over to where his mom and sister are sitting)* Uh, Ellen. What can I do? I'd like to help.

**Ellen:** Just pray, Toby. Pray.

**Toby:** *(goes back by the tree)* Dear Jesus, I need a favor tonight. My friend, Taylor, is hurt, bad. I know we fight a lot and all, but I like her. Would you please help her? Thanks. Amen.

*(Robert and Jack enter as Toby finishes.)*

**Robert:** We're back. Any change yet?

**Annie:** *(runs to Jack)* Not yet, I'm afraid.

**Jack:** *(looks at all those in the house)* Oh, I'm sorry. Hey, I know you might want to be somewhere else ...

**Bertram:** *(interrupts)* There is no place we'd rather be, Mr. Hanson. When Mr. Crandle told us, we knew what we must do.

**Mr. Crandle:** They made me bring 'em here, Mr. Hanson. They wouldn't take "No" for an answer.

**Mrs. Firkins:** Mr. Hanson, we're praying for you and Taylor. We love you.

**Claire:** That's right, Jack.

**Maudie:** We've come to pray.

**Pastor Olson:** We're family, Jack, and that's what families do.

**Jack:** *(moved by the sentiment of his friends)* Thank you, thank you all. We need to pray. Won't you join me?

*(All stand and form a circle and Jack starts to pray. Robert, though, slips away into the bedroom.)*

**Robert:** Uh, doc. I'll sit here for you for a few minutes.

**Dr. Leland:** Sure. Thanks, Robert.

*(Dr. Leland leaves. Robert is alone in the room with Taylor.)*

**Robert:** *(speaks to God as he sits by Taylor's bed)* Uh, God. I know I haven't been the father I should have. I have a son and daughter that I barely know. But, I'm coming to you to ask a favor. I don't deserve it, but it's not for me. It's for my son. Could you give him back his little girl? I don't know how to say it any better than that. He is a good dad and he loves her. Please, God, please.

*(While Robert prays, he lays his head on Taylor's bed. As he concludes the prayer, he weeps quietly. Taylor's hand comes up to pat her grandfather.)*

**Taylor:** Don't cry.

**Robert:** What? What did you say?

**Taylor:** Don't cry. It will be all right.

**Robert:** *(ecstatically)* All right? It is more than all right. *(calls to the living room)* Come! Quick!

*(Robert is joined by Jack, Annie, and Martha. Dr. Leland also comes in to check on Taylor.)*

**Martha:** It's a miracle.

**Annie:** It's an answer to our prayers.

**Jack:** Yes, Annie. It sure is.

The End

# A Christmas Remembrance

A Multigenerational
Christmas Drama
With An Order Of Worship

## Arthur J. L. Meether

# A Christmas Remembrance

**Characters**
    Narrator
    Elder
    Julia
    Theodotus and his family
    Member One
    Child One
    Member Two (adult)
    Member Three
    Samuel
    Child Two
    Stephen
    Child's Mother
    Junius
    Man
    Tychicus
    Choir or Singing Group
    Sunday School Members
    Child Three
    Child Four
    Child Five
    Child Six
    Child Seven
    Child Eight
    Child Nine
    Child Ten
    Child Eleven
    Child Twelve
    Member Four
    Member Five

**Setting**
    The setting is an open room. The only furniture is a low table. It is a place where Christians meet for worship about the year 70 AD. The room is empty at first, but fills as worshipers arrive.

---

**Organ Prelude**

**Processional Carol**                                                        "O Come, All Ye Faithful"

**The Introit**

Leader: God's time to fulfill man's redemptive needs, as he had promised through the prophets, had come.

**People: The Logos, that is the ruling power of the universe, became a human being and lived among us.**

Leader: Out of the fullness of his grace he blessed us all, giving us one blessing after another.

**People: God gave the law through Moses; but grace and truth came through Jesus Christ.**

Leader: No one has ever seen God.

**People: The only one who is the same as God and is at the Father's side, he has made him known.**

**Hymn**                                                                       "I Am So Glad, Each Christmas Eve"

### The Christmas Drama

**Narrator:** The year is 70 AD, that is about forty years after the crucifixion of Christ. The setting is in a small village in Asia Minor where local Christians are about to gather for worship. Their leader, or elder, arrives first to prepare for services. A deaconess joins him, bringing bread and wine for the love feast; shortly, others arrive singly or in family groups.

**Elder:** Shalom. Peace be with you, Julia. It is good you can be with us tonight.

**Julia:** I have told my master about Jesus. He does not yet believe, but I pray for him. He knows how much Christ means to me, and he has told me that I may always have free time to worship.

**Elder:** May God bless him for his generosity and bring him to know the truth.

*(Theodotus and his family enter.)*

**Elder and Julia:** *(together)* Peace be with you, brother Theodotus. May God's grace rest on you and your family.

**Theodotus and Family:** Peace be with you, also.

**Julia:** *(sets the bread and wine on the table)* Do you think there will be enough? The caravan from Ephesus is back. We may have many tonight.

**Elder:** Do not be concerned. The Lord will provide. Another brother or sister will come with a bit more bread and wine.

**Theodotus:** I understand you will be reading tonight from the new scroll that you just got from Ephesus yesterday. Is this another letter by the apostle Paul?

**Elder:** No, brother. This is something new and different. The brothers in Ephesus call it a gospel. They told me that they got their copy from Antioch and are making copies for all the congregations around here when papyrus can be obtained. It is so expensive, and we have so few who are able to copy scroll.

**Member One:** If it is not by Paul, who wrote it?

**Elder:** I asked them who had prepared it, but they did not know for sure. The man who brought the copy from Antioch said that the people down there had heard it said that the writer is a fellow named Mark who used to go around with Paul and also with Peter. It is hard to say about these things. We have to be so careful lest the wrong people hear about our meetings and then you well know what can happen. If it were not for this, it would be possible to check these things out better. The teaching agrees, though, with what I heard from the lips of the blessed Paul.

*(People have been coming in singly and by families and squatting on the floor around the table during the conversation. One or another brings a bit of wine or bread and puts it on the table.)*

**Child One:** Does the new scroll tell us anything about when Jesus was born or when he was a child?

**Elder:** Almost nothing. The scroll does tell us that his mother, Mary, his brothers and sisters, as well as the townspeople of Nazareth, did not believe in him when he first began to preach. His family even tried to take him in charge to prevent him from preaching. This seems to tell us that his early life must have been quite ordinary.

**Theodotus:** Remember, little one — his birth is not like his ministry, his death, and resurrection. These things happened in my lifetime and in the elder's lifetime. We talked to the people who saw the risen Lord and heard their testimony. His birth was seventy or eighty years ago. All the adults who were alive then are dead by now. So it would be hard to find out information about his birth and childhood.

**Member Two:** Can you read us those portions of the scroll tonight that you mentioned?

**Elder:** Indeed, I can. It looks like we are all here, so perhaps we should start. I will first read from the new scroll. Then as we have a number of our members back with us from a journey, we can ask them if they have heard anything about the birth and childhood of Jesus from the brothers and sisters they may have met on their travels.

The new scroll says, "Then he went home; and the crowd came together again, so that they could not even eat. When his family heard it, they went out to restrain him, for people were saying, 'He has gone out of his mind.' ... Then his mother and his brother came; and standing outside, they sent to him and called him. A crowd was sitting around him; and they said to him, 'Your mother and your brothers and sisters are outside, asking for you.' And he replied, 'Who are my mother and my brothers?' And looking at those who sat around him, he said, 'Here are my mother and my brothers! Whoever does the will of God is my brother and sister and mother.' ... He left that place and came to his hometown, and his disciples followed him. On the sabbath he began to teach in the synagogue, and many who heard him were astonished. They said, 'Where did this man get all this? What is this wisdom that has been given to him? What deeds of power are being done by his hands! Is not this the carpenter, the son of Mary and brother of James and Joses and Judas and Simon, and are not his sisters here with us?' And they took offense at him. Then Jesus said to them, 'Prophets are not without honor, except in their hometown, and among their own kin, and in their own house.' And he could do no deed of power there, except that he laid his hands on a few sick people and cured them" (Mark 3:20-21, 31-35; 6:1-5).

**Member Two:** How strange that even his closest relatives and family did not believe in him and even tried to stop him from preaching!

**Member Three:** We must remember that not even the disciples fully understood him until after God raised him from the dead. His mother and his family also came to faith at a later time. Samuel here has a story about the birth of Jesus that he heard among some of the brothers south of us when he visited with them. Won't you tell it to us, Samuel?

**Elder:** Yes, please do.

**Samuel:** According to what I was told, Jesus' mother, Mary, was visited by a heavenly messenger and the messenger told her, "Don't be afraid, Mary, because God has been gracious to you. You will become pregnant and give birth to a son and you will call him Jesus. He will be great and will be called the Son of the Most High God. The Lord God will make him a king, as his ancestor David was, and he will be king of the descendants of Jacob forever; his kingdom will never end."

**Child One:** What a wonderful story. Is there more to it?

**Samuel:** That is about all I remember. Oh yes, I remember they said that Mary was very happy and believed it would be as the messenger said. Later on when she visited her cousin, she sang a beautiful song of praise.

**Hymn** "The Magnificat"

**Child Two:** What do heavenly messengers look like? Can you tell us, Mr. Samuel?

**Samuel:** Well, I have never seen one. I have never talked with anyone who has. I asked a rabbi who taught me the law as a boy. He thought they would be like very strong men — would probably wear armor and carry weapons and look very fierce. Perhaps the elder can help us. He was taught by a famous rabbi.

**Elder:** I do not know, either. Our new scroll describes a messenger seen by the women at the empty tomb as a "youth in a white robe." They must look much like ordinary humans. Do you have any more information you can give us, Samuel?

**Samuel:** I have heard another story about Jesus' birth from our brother, Stephen. He is here tonight. I think it would be best if he would tell it to us. It is a story about how Jesus came to be born in Bethlehem.

*(The elder nods his approval to Stephen who rises to tell his story. As Stephen tells his story a manger with Mary and Joseph characters by it is assembled in the foreground and the smaller members of the Sunday school quietly gather around it.)*

**Stephen:** Jesus was born at a time when the Romans were taking a census. Joseph, a carpenter of Nazareth, had to go to Bethlehem to register because he was of Davidic descent. The girl he was engaged to was Mary. Though Mary was pregnant, Joseph took her with him to the registration. The town of Bethlehem was so crowded when they got there that they had to stay in a stable. And that is where Jesus was born. His mother wrapped him in swaddling clothes and laid him in a manger.

**Child Two:** Just like me. I was born right by the animals just like Ruth and Saul and Jesus, too.

**Child's Mother:** Hush, child. Some inns where rich people go have separate stables. Not everyone keeps their animals right in the house with them like we do.

**Hymn** "Away In A Manger"
*(Sung by smaller Sunday school children gathered around the manger.)*

**Junius:** I heard tell about how some shepherds visited the baby Jesus in Bethlehem. Would you like to hear the story? *(Pauses to get a response. The members of the gathered congregation nod their approval.)* Some heavenly messengers appeared to some shepherds tending their flocks in the fields near Bethlehem and told them about Jesus' birth. Indeed, it is said that the shepherds heard a whole army of heavenly messengers singing, "Glory to God in the highest heaven and peace on earth to those with whom he is pleased." They went to the stable and visited the newborn Savior and his parents and found things as the messengers had told them.

**Hymn** "What Child Is This?"

**Elder:** Well, it seems we do have a few traditions about our Lord's birth after all. Are there any more?

**Man:** Yes, Tychicus. You have a tradition to share?

**Tychicus:** I can tell you a story about the visit of some magi to our Lord.

**The Group:** *(all murmur and several speak out at once)* Magi! Those rogues! They are star worshipers! What can heathens like that have to do with our Lord?

**Tychicus:** I know the reputation of the magi well. I put no store by their teaching that they can read the future of all our lives in the stars. I didn't invent the story, however. Do you want to hear it or not?

**Elder:** Our Lord received tax collectors and prostitutes in his great mercy. He called the persecutor Saul to be the apostle Paul. Is it not possible that he also received some magi? Let us hear the tradition.

**Sunday School Members:** Amen. Let us hear it.

**Tychicus:** According to the story I received that I now pass on to you, some magi came to Jerusalem to Herod who was king then, asking to see the one who was born King of the Jews. They said that they had learned about this from their study of the stars. Herod was upset because the last thing he wanted around was a rival king. He checked with his experts who told him that the Messiah, the anointed one, was to be born in Bethlehem. He gave this information to the magi and asked them to come back and let him know where the Messiah was. They went, found the baby, worshiped him, and gave him presents of gold, frankincense, and myrrh. God warned them about Herod's intentions to kill the child in a dream, however, so they slipped out of the country without reporting back to him.

**Choir or Singing Group:** *(sings)* "We Three Kings Of Orient Are"
*(The manger group with the younger Sunday school pupils around it has remained in the foreground until now.)*

**Younger Sunday School Member:** *(sings)* "What Can I Give Him?"
*(Only the first line is sung with piano accompaniment or guitar until all spoken lines are finished.)*

**All:** *(sing)* **What can I give him, poor as I am?**

**Spoken parts:**

**Child One:** If I were a shepherd, I could bring a lamb.

**Child Two:** If I were a rich man, I would give gifts of gold, silver, and fine clothes.

**Child Three:** If I were a king, I would give him my protection.

**All:** *(sing)* **What can I give him, poor as I am?**

**Child Four:** I can give him my attention. I can hear his teaching and live by it.

**Child Five:** I can love other people in the same way that Jesus has loved me.

**Child Six:** I can love and honor my dear parents who first told me of him and brought me to baptism.

**All:** *(sing)* **What can I give him, poor as I am?**

**Child Seven:** I can give him money from my allowance to feed and clothe those who need help.

**Child Eight:** I can tell my friends about him; how he loves us all and will take care of us whether we live or whether we die.

**Child Nine:** I can praise and worship God as he taught us to do.

**All:** *(sing)* **What can I give him, poor as I am?**

**Child Ten:** I can be a friend to someone who is lonely.

**Child Eleven:** I can visit someone who is ill and can pray for him.

**Child Twelve:** I can study hard and learn more about him so I can explain to others why we believe and trust in the Lord Jesus.

*(The smaller children now sing the whole song. The manger scene is taken away and the younger ones resume their places in the Sunday school congregation.)*

**Elder:** All these things are interesting to hear. Perhaps, someday, someone will write these stories down on a scroll for us. However, I do not even remember the blessed Paul mentioning any of these things. Not even on one occasion. Possibly, he was too concerned with teaching us the way of salvation to tell us of those matters. Maybe he did not know of these things. Let us now recall those things that stand at the very heart of our faith and hope as taught to us by the Lord's apostles.

*(Elder now nods to various members in turn.)*

**Member One:** *(rises)* The prophets spoke of one whom God would send. He has come in the person of our Lord Jesus Christ.

**Member Two:** *(rises)* Paul asserted as of greatest importance: Christ died for our sins as written in the scriptures; he was buried and God raised him to life on the third day as promised in the scriptures; he appeared alive to Peter, then to the twelve apostles, and eventually to more than 500 people, and finally also to our own apostle Paul.

**Member Three:** *(rises)* Christ has returned to the Father and into full use of the divine power by which he rules all things for our God.

**Member Four:** *(rises)* Christ is present among us through the Holy Spirit who works in us and gives us power.

**Member Five:** *(rises)* Jesus will come again at a time not disclosed to us to bring the present age to an end and to raise the dead and give eternal life and happiness to all who trust in him.

**Elder:** And because all of this is true, what are we to instruct all men to do?

**All: Turn about and get a fresh start! Admit our wrongdoing and be baptized. If we do so, God will forgive us and give us everlasting life.**

**Elder:** Now, let us remember all these things that our Lord has done for us in the way that he has asked his own to remember him.

**All: From our Lord we receive the teaching that our Lord Jesus, on the night he was betrayed, took bread** *(Elder takes the loaves and breaks them)*, **gave thanks, broke it, and gave it to his disciples, saying, "Take, eat, this is my body, which is given for you. Do this in remembrance of me." In the same way, he took the cup** *(Elder takes the cup)*, **and gave it to them saying, "Drink of it, all of you; this is my blood of the new covenant, which is poured out for you for the forgiveness of sins. Do this, as often as you drink it, in remembrance of me."**

**Sunday School:** *(sings)* "I Am The Resurrection And The Life"

**Elder:** *(distributes the bread)* We thank you, Father, for life and the knowledge you have made known to us through Jesus, your Son. Glory be yours forever. Just as this bread was once one loaf, so let all your people who join in this feast be gathered together as one into your kingdom.

**Sunday School:** Christ has died, Christ has risen, Christ will come again.

**Elder:** *(passes the cup)* We thank you, Father, for the holy vine of your servant, David, which you have made known to us through your Son Jesus. Glory to you forever.

**Sunday School:** Christ has died, Christ his risen, Christ will come again. Amen. Come, Lord Jesus.

**Hymn** "Go Tell It On The Mountain"

**Elder:** The grace of the Lord Jesus Christ, the love of God and the fellowship of the Holy Spirit be with you and abide with you forever.

**Sunday School:** Amen.

**Hymn** "Silent Night"
*(Sunday school marches out during the singing of the last verse of this hymn.)*

# Christmas, Then And Now: As Witnessed By The Angels

A One-Act Christmas Drama
For Adults Or Older Youth

## Robert V. Dodd

*Based on an original work by Elizabeth P. Armstrong

*This work is dedicated to the glory of God
in loving memory of Lewis D. Armstrong and Elizabeth P. Armstrong,
who developed its first draft.*

# Preface

  This drama was originally written by my mother-in-law, Elizabeth Patten Armstrong, and initially performed in the 1980s at her home church, Christ United Methodist Church, in Wilmington, Delaware. As a dedicated Christian, she expressed her devotion to Christ through her love of family, her support of the church, and her involvement in the ministry of the church, eagerly serving in whatever capacity the opportunity afforded. In that capacity, she served as a Sunday school teacher and a church officer. She was a devoted wife and mother of two daughters. She and her husband, Lewis D. Armstrong, were married for over 59 years. Among her other gifts and talents, she was an excellent seamstress and cook, who used all of her abilities to glorify God and to bless others. To my knowledge, this was the only drama that she ever wrote.

  With the permission of her daughters, Ann and Valerie, I have taken her original idea and updated and expanded it in order to make it more suitable for a contemporary audience. I believe that in doing so, I have been able to preserve most of her original intent, namely to bring glory to God through the celebration of the birth of God's Son, our Savior and Lord Jesus Christ.

— Robert V. Dodd

# Christmas, Then And Now: As Witnessed By The Angels

**Production Notes**

Two angels, Michael and Gabriel, are assigned to stand watch on the night that Jesus was born and discuss what they see. On Christmas Eve of this year, the same two angels are assigned to stand watch again. They discuss what they have witnessed, and also the similarities and differences between the way Jesus' birth was first observed and the way it is celebrated today.

This one-act drama will help participants and listeners have a better understanding of what actually happened on the night the Savior was born and the importance of that event. It clears up a lot of misunderstanding concerning the events surrounding Jesus' birth and how Christmas should be celebrated today.

The audience will be helped to understand why Joseph and Mary were in Bethlehem on that first Christmas Eve, why their spending the night in a stable may have actually been better accommodations than the inn, why it may have taken the wise men or magi as long as two years to find the Christ Child, why the angels who spoke to the shepherds did not sing, but rather chanted or shouted, and why we celebrate Jesus' birth on December 25, when he was likely born in either April or September.

There are two main characters on stage, dressed in white robes and tinsel, simulating halos. Wings are optional. Several offstage voices have brief speaking parts. There is also the opportunity for solos, instrumentals, choirs, and congregational singing as deemed necessary.

This presentation requires minimal costume design, no special scenery or props, and simple lighting. It would be appropriate for use in a Sunday morning or evening worship service, or as a simple but profound afternoon or evening program. Presentation time is approximately twenty minutes, depending upon the number of musical selections. It can be performed as a play or as a dramatic reading and has the potential to involve as many people as desired.

**Characters**
 Narrator
 Angel Gabriel
 Angel Michael
 Voice Of Third Angel (offstage)
 Voices Of Several Angels (offstage)
 Voice Of Micah (offstage)
 Voice Of Mary (offstage)
 Voice Of Jesus (offstage)
 Voice Of God (offstage)

**Crews**
 Sound
 Lighting
 Musical Director(s) and Musicians
 Soloists and Choirs

**Note:** In addition to the two main characters, Gabriel and Michael, a variety of people can be used to provide the various characters' voices and to serve as technical assistants, or several of those responsibilities can be handled by the same individuals. Thus, these roles can be creatively overlapped or distributed in order to accommodate the number of people available.

---

**Narrator:** This one-act play consists of conversations between two angels, Michael and Gabriel, who were assigned to be on watch on the night that our Savior was born, some 2,000 years ago, and then again on Christmas Eve of this year. It could be a little difficult to imagine the participants as the angels, Michael and Gabriel, because you know them as your friends and fellow church members. To help with the illusion, they will wear white robes and garlands of tinsel in their hair to simulate halos. You will also notice that they have neither harp nor trumpet to play. They will not be furnishing tonight's music. You and the others will be doing that, as we join in singing some familiar Christmas carols to set the mood for our play.

*(Here several Christmas carols may be sung by the congregation, or special music by the adult, hand bell, and children's choirs may be used. The hymn, "Silent Night," may be sung as a solo or as a congregational hymn, or simply played on piano, organ, or flute, immediately prior to the beginning of the play.)*

### Scene One
### On The Occasion Of The First Christmas

*(The middle of the stage is illuminated by a spotlight or floodlight and otherwise darkened. Two angels enter from opposite sides of the stage and meet in the center.)*

**Michael:** Good evening, Gabriel. This is the night that we have all been waiting for — the night when the Savior is born. O holy night! What cause for rejoicing! What a night to be on watch.

**Gabriel:** Yes. Down through the ages, this is the night all heaven and earth has been anticipating. And now it is here! Tonight we are going to witness the unfolding of the greatest drama in human history, foretold by their prophets hundreds and hundreds of years ago.

**Michael:** *(points offstage to his right)* Look over there near Bethlehem. It's already beginning to happen. Those two people, Mary and Joseph, are entering the city of Bethlehem. Joseph is leading the donkey on which his soon-to-be wife, Mary, is riding. She looks pale and tired and very pregnant. It is a long trip from Nazareth to Bethlehem. Gabriel, tell me something. Did you ever ride on a donkey?

**Gabriel:** No. I can't say that I have ever ridden a donkey. I don't think it would be very comfortable, especially if you were pregnant. But then again, I wouldn't know anything about that either, being an angel and all. I do think that if I had to travel that far, I would prefer using my wings. That is if I were wearing my wings at the time. After all, they are a lot faster and a more efficient form of transportation.

**Michael:** Joseph is going into the inn now to get a place for them to stay for the night. You know, Gabriel, I always wondered how the Christ Child could be born in Bethlehem when Mary and Joseph lived in Nazareth.

**Gabriel:** It was the prophet, Micah, who announced the place of his birth.

**Voice Of Micah:** But you, O Bethlehem of Ephrathah, who are one of the little clans of Judah, from you shall come forth for me one who is to rule Israel, whose origin is from old, from ancient days (Micah 5:2).

**Gabriel:** Caesar Augustus unknowingly gave full meaning to Micah's prophecy when he decreed that all the world under Roman authority should be taxed. In order for this taxation to take place, he had a census taken to record the origins of the people. Every male human had to enroll in the city of his birth. Since Joseph was from the city of Bethlehem, he went there to register and took Mary with him. She was ready to have her baby any day — or night. That's why the Savior was born in Bethlehem. Isn't it wonderful how the Lord God often uses some of the most unlikely people to accomplish his purposes?

**Michael:** Yes, it is. God has resources at his disposal that even angels fail to understand. *(pauses, as if thinking about what he will say next)* I wonder, was it difficult for you to tell Mary of God's plan for her when God sent you on that divine mission? After all, it was such a delicate matter, her not being married and all.

**Gabriel:** It was, to say the least, a very delicate matter. I appreciated the confidence that the Lord had placed in me and did the best that I could, angelically speaking, to explain God's plan to her. Mary was frightened when she first saw me. I suppose angels are an awesome and fearful sight to humans.

**Michael:** *(excitedly interrupts)* And it isn't every day that young teenage girls see angels.

**Gabriel:** I suppose it isn't. But, I told Mary not to be afraid. That seemed to calm her fears somewhat. I then said that the Lord God had sent me to tell her that she had been honored and set apart from all women on earth. She had been chosen to conceive and give birth to the one who would be Savior of the world. She was still puzzled. But after that, her face started to glow and she responded wonderfully. *(pauses for a moment and looks down, then looks at Michael again)*

Of course, she had some questions that still needed to be answered, like how this could possibly happen, since she was not married. But I told her this was God's doing and that the Holy Spirit would come upon her and the child conceived in her womb would be called Holy Lord, Son of God, and Prince of Peace. I'll never forget the look on her face when she responded.

**Voice Of Mary:** Here am I, the servant of the Lord; let it be with me according to your word (Luke 1:38).

**Gabriel:** I also told Mary that if she needed further assurance, she should know that her cousin, Elizabeth, who was often called barren because she couldn't have children, had conceived and was in the third month of her pregnancy, even though she was well past the age of having children.

Since they didn't have telephones or email or anything like those communication devices future generations will invent, I encouraged Mary to visit Elizabeth and find out for herself the truth of all that I had told her. You should have heard her explain to Elizabeth what had happened.

**Voice Of Mary:** My soul magnifies the Lord, and my spirit rejoices in God my Savior, for he has looked with favor on the lowliness of his servant. Surely, from now on all generations will call me blessed; for the Mighty One has done great things for me, and holy is his name. His mercy is for those who fear him from generation to generation (Luke 1:47-50).

**Michael:** And what about Joseph? I know that he must have loved Mary. After all, they were engaged to be married. Didn't he have some doubts concerning Mary's explanation of her pregnancy? Didn't he feel betrayed in some way?

**Gabriel:** Yes, of course he did. But Joseph was a fair and righteous man. He had mixed feelings about what had happened to Mary and how he should respond. He truly loved Mary, and his heart was nearly broken by what he thought was her betrayal of their love. But then, I appeared to him in a dream and explained to him that Mary's child was a holy child, the product of God's action and love. I also reassured him that he should not be reluctant to take Mary to be his wife and that she had always been faithful to him, and always would be.

**Michael:** *(points to the right side of the stage)* Joseph is coming out of the inn now. He is shaking his head as if puzzled. He is explaining to Mary that there is no room for them in the inn — no place for them to spread their pallets and lie down for the night. There are people sleeping everywhere, all over the floor. And it is also smelly, because many of them brought their animals inside with them to prevent them from being stolen. This is not unusual for the inns in this day and time, but it does present a crowded, noisy, smelly environment. Certainly no place for the Savior to be born. What are they going to do? Where will they go?

**Gabriel:** Just watch and listen. Joseph is explaining to Mary that the innkeeper suggested a clean, quiet, and private place better suited for them to sleep, just in case her baby was born that night. The innkeeper said they could stay in the stable for the night if they wanted. The stable is behind the inn and carved into the limestone cliffs. It's quiet and clean, with fresh straw for them and the donkey. Mary is very tired and needs to rest. So, she and Joseph have decided to stay in the stable. It's better than the crowded inn. Maybe tomorrow they can find other accommodations.

**Michael:** This time of the year in the hills around Bethlehem, shepherds take their sheep out to feed on the tender new grass in the spring pastures. There are some shepherds gathered around a campfire. They are watching their sheep tonight and protecting them from predators and thieves. There is a strange silence, a kind of hush over the earth, as if nature itself is anticipating some great event that is about to take place. The sheep seem rather restless and uneasy. Even the shepherds are more alert than usual.

**Gabriel:** *(looks up)* Oh, I see why. It's that star! *(points toward the ceiling)* Just look at it. Have you ever seen such a brilliant star? Star of wonder, star of light, star of beauty shining bright. Its beam appears to reach down all the way to the earth.

**Michael:** Look, Gabriel. There is another angel of the Lord approaching the shepherds. Listen to what he is saying.

**Voice Of Third Angel:** Do not be afraid; for see — I am bringing you good news of great joy for all the people: to you is born this day in the city of David a Savior, who is the Messiah, the Lord. This will be a sign for you: you will find a child wrapped in bands of cloth and lying in a manger (Luke 2:10-12).

**Michael:** Now there is a whole gathering of angels, an angelic chorus, surrounding the shepherds and shouting.

**Voices Of Several Angels:** Glory to God in the highest heaven, and on earth peace among those he favors! (Luke 2:14).

**Michael:** The angels are returning to heaven. And the shepherds are talking among themselves about going to Bethlehem to look for this baby who was born to be the Savior of the world. The Child that the angels told them about would be wrapped in bands of cloth, which is their custom, and lying in a manger — an animal's feeding trough, at exactly the time they would find him. Imagine that!

**Gabriel:** I can hear one young shepherd saying that he cannot go. One of his lambs is missing and he must stay in the hills to look for it. Others say they're too tired to make the trip. But some of the more adventuresome shepherds decide to go into the city and look for the Holy Child. Watching over sheep is often a boring task anyway. I imagine that they could use some mystery and excitement in their lives.

**Michael:** Shepherding sheep must get kind of boring at times. Especially during the night while the sheep are sleeping. But the shepherds have to stay awake and alert to protect their sheep from predators.

**Gabriel:** The shepherds who went into the city are asking different people about the birth of a baby in a stable this night. The angel's description of a baby gave them a clue that the birth would take place in a stable. They're going all over Bethlehem asking, "Has anyone seen or heard about a baby being born in a stable tonight?"

**Michael:** Look! They're entering a simple stable, carved out of limestone in a cliff behind the inn. They can't believe their eyes. There's the baby wrapped in strips of cloth and lying in a manger just like the angels said he would be. They stand there in awe and wonder.

**Gabriel:** Several of them are getting down on their knees. Some of them are telling Mary and Joseph about their vision of angels and the angels' chorus, "Glory to God in the highest heaven, and on earth peace among those whom he favors!" Mary and Joseph thank them. One of the shepherds says, "Look, the baby is smiling at us." His smile fills their hearts with joy and peace.

**Michael:** Now, the shepherds are returning to their flocks in the hills. But there is a lightness in their steps and they're turning to their work with renewed energy and hope. The angels' voices are still ringing in their ears and in their hearts, "Glory to God in the highest!" I don't think work will ever be boring for them again.

**Gabriel:** Me, either. Well, dawn is upon us, Michael. We must return to heaven. Our tour of duty on earth is over. We have witnessed the Savior's birth. We are truly blessed, even among the angels. All praise to God!

**Michael:** One thing bothers me. One of the greatest events in human history has taken place this night and nobody but a few shepherds seemed to notice. Hundreds of years later, a hymn writer named Phillips Brooks will write, "How silently, how silently, the wondrous gift is given; so God imparts to human hearts the blessings of his heaven ..." ("O Little Town Of Bethlehem").

**Gabriel:** Yes, many of God's miracles are of a less spectacular nature so that they are only seen through the eyes of faith. But the rest of us can still praise God and shout, "Glory to God in the highest."

**Michael:** Yes, let us all praise God and shout, "Glory to God in the highest!"

*(Both angels exit to the left of the stage together.)*

*(A Christmas carol, solo, or other musical arrangement can be featured at this time.)*

### Scene Two
### Christmas, This Year

**Michael:** Gabriel, it has been a long time in earth years since we were on watch duty the night when the Savior was born, but only a few minutes have passed in terms of eternity. My, how things have changed! The human race has multiplied — quadrupled — quintupled many times over. People have spread out over the entire planet and civilizations have risen and fallen since the Savior's birth. Human beings have created many wonderful inventions like the automobile, the train, and the airplane.

**Gabriel:** Then there's the invention of the transistor, the silicone chip, and the worldwide web. The splitting of the atom has been both a blessing and a curse. Advances have been made in medicine, surgery, diagnosis, treatment of disease, and medical technology.

**Michael:** Human beings have even landed on the moon. Now they're sending unmanned space ships to other planets. What next? Knowledge abounds and humans have discovered so many things that were formerly known only to God.

**Gabriel:** We could spend all night talking about the discoveries and inventions that have changed the way humans live. They can now communicate from one end of the earth to the other in a matter of seconds. Only prayer is a faster means of communication than that. God once promised ...

**Voice Of God:** Before they call I will answer, while they are yet speaking I will hear (Isaiah 65:24).

**Michael:** Now that's what I call fast.

**Gabriel:** Whatever happened to the "peace on earth among those whom God favors" that those angels talked about on the night when they announced the Savior's birth to the shepherds? The United States has been involved in wars with Japan, Germany, North Korea, and Vietnam. There have also been wars in Bosnia, Kosovo, Iran, Iraq, Liberia, and in Somalia.

**Michael:** The threat of terrorism exists all around the world. Even the United States is not immune, as the events of 9-11-01 demonstrated. Adolf Hitler, Mussolini, Slobodan Milosevic, Osama bin Laden, and Saddam Hussein have proven how very low humanity can go. Then there's famine, poverty, and the spread of the HIV virus that causes AIDS.

**Gabriel:** And don't forget crimes, robberies, and murders are everywhere you look. I sometimes wonder what God sees in these humans. What is it that gives them their dignity and worth?

**Michael:** The true worth of something is determined by the price that is paid for it. The Son of God gave his very life for these humans. Doesn't that make them of infinite worth to God?

**Gabriel:** Yes, of course, you're right.

**Michael:** Gabriel, perhaps you are looking for peace in the wrong places. Before there can be the kind of peace that you are talking about, there must be peace in the hearts of all humankind, the peace that only the Lord Jesus can give. He once said ...

**Voice Of Jesus:** Peace I leave with you; my peace I give to you. I do not give to you as the world gives. Do not let your hearts be troubled, and do not let them be afraid (John 14:27).

**Michael:** There is peace on earth, but it is only in the hearts of true believers in the Lord Jesus. However, there is not enough of them to make a complete difference in the world. At least not yet!

**Gabriel:** On the night that Jesus was born, there were shepherds keeping watch over their sheep in the new spring pastures of the Judean hills. So why do people celebrate the Savior's birth on December 25 in the middle of winter?

**Michael:** Because that is three days following the shortest day of the year. As the days begin to get longer and the nights shorter, people are reminded that an even greater light has come into the world that will dispel all spiritual darkness. Three days and the light is gradually returning to overpower the night. Jesus rose from the dead on the third day. Get it?

**Gabriel:** That makes sense. But Christmas Eve is so different now. Instead of the quietness that marked the first Christmas Eve, there is such busyness, such a flurry of activity. Christians and non-Christians get into the act with so much shopping to do, so many cookies to bake, so many cards to write, so many presents to wrap, and so much decorating to do. Christmas has gone commercial. The merchants love it. They depend on it to make a profit for the year. Indeed, the day after Thanksgiving is now called Black Friday. It is the day when merchants are said to get out of the red and into the black for the first time all year, thanks to Christmas sales. And really, for many it has become a holiday instead of a *holy* day.

**Michael:** Some people even refuse to refer to it as the Christmas season. They want to call it the holiday season.

**Gabriel:** Don't they know that the word "holiday" comes from the two words "holy" and "day"? The Christmas holiday is supposed to be a holy day. The Christmas season is supposed to be a holy season.

**Michael:** How quickly they forget. *(pauses for a moment, then points)* Look at all those chocolate-chip cookies being baked. Did you ever see so many? There are also sugar cookies, brownies, and lemon squares ...

**Gabriel:** *(interrupts)* and peanut butter cookies and oatmeal cookies.

**Michael:** *(excitedly)* Don't forget those delicious homemade fruitcakes.

**Gabriel:** How about that commercially prepared and packaged fruitcake that keeps on being passed around from person to person and year to year. I wonder how old it is and why it doesn't spoil. No one ever eats it, but they always express thanks for it.

**Michael:** It's called a tradition. Gabriel, have you ever been tempted to taste one of those earthly morsels?

**Gabriel:** Well, not exactly. But I have often wondered whether they are as good as angel food.

**Michael:** Then, there's the matter of gift giving. Those wise men really started something when they came to present their gifts of gold, frankincense, and myrrh to the Christ Child and his earthly parents.

**Gabriel:** It certainly took them a long time to find the Holy Family — almost two years. But, I guess that is to be expected. It takes time to organize a caravan and to purchase supplies for a long journey.

**Michael:** After all, they were following a new star in the sky. Finally, they asked King Herod if he knew anything about the birth of a new king. They thought that surely the present king would be aware of the birth of his successor. The strange thing about it all is that today people give gifts to each other, instead of to the Christ Child. Look at those gifts down there under the Christmas tree. Can you read the names on them?

**Gabriel:** Yes, that large one is for *(name someone in the audience)*. That funny-shaped one is for *(name someone else in the audience)*. That very small one is for *(name someone else)*. And the one that is too big to wrap is for *(name a final person)*.

**Michael:** Do you see any marked for Jesus? It's his birthday, you know.

**Gabriel:** No, I don't. But, wait a minute. There are some gifts under the Chrismon *(or Angel)* tree that people have been putting there every Sunday in Advent. There is food for the hungry. There are toys for needy children and clothes for children and adults. Then there are all those charitable concerns that the church supports at Christmas, like *(name some of the helping organizations and causes your church supports)*.

**Michael:** Oh, I get it. These are all gifts for Jesus, because he said ...

**Voice Of Jesus:** Truly I tell you, just as you did it to one of the least of these who are members of my family, you did it to me (Matthew 25:40).

**Michael:** Yes, these are all gifts for Jesus, and so is the money dropped in the Salvation Army kettles, and clothing given to Goodwill, cookies baked for nursing home residents, and hundreds of other acts of kindness that are worth far more than the monetary value attached to them.

**Gabriel:** You know, Michael, my guess is that if all the money that was spent selfishly at Christmas had been used to pay off the national debt, the United States would be in a lot better shape financially.

**Michael:** Better still, if that money was used to proclaim the gospel around the world, the whole world would be in much better shape in every way. Have you noticed all those Nativity scenes scattered over the countryside? Saint Francis of Assisi was the first to present such a scene way back in the thirteenth century. It was in a cave in Italy. He used real people except for the baby Jesus and real animals, too. People came from all the neighboring villages to stare in awe and rethink the birth of Christ.

**Gabriel:** There are many such scenes on earth tonight, some very simple and some rather elaborate.

**Michael:** I know of one Nativity scene that graces the mantle in a certain home. It is there because once there was a little girl who said all she wanted for Christmas was a Nativity scene. Her parents bought her the nicest gift they could afford and gave it to her for Christmas. It made them all so very happy. After Christmas it was carefully wrapped and put away until the next year. This was done year after year, until the girl grew up to become a woman who got married and had children and now has grandchildren. Every Christmas she takes out that very special gift and puts it in a prominent place on her mantle for everyone to enjoy.

**Gabriel:** But, Michael, do you know that in many instances today Nativity scenes are banned in public places and on government property? They call it separation of church and state. They do not understand that in the kingdom of God, there is no such thing. God is all and in all. No wonder Jesus taught his disciples to pray ...

**Voice Of Jesus:** Your kingdom come. Your will be done, on earth as it is in heaven (Matthew 6:10).

**Michael:** Even so, Gabriel, in spite of all the myths and legends and traditions, things that were not present at that first Christmas, like Santa Claus, hanging stockings, Christmas trees, Rudolph the red-nosed reindeer, holly and mistletoe, the colors red and green, lights and candles and even more lights, all these things, there is something about the way Earth now celebrates Christmas that is true to the real spirit of Christmas.

**Gabriel:** What is it, Michael?

**Michael:** It is the music and songs of Christmas. There are such lovely ones, like "Silent Night," "O Little Town Of Bethlehem," or "It Came Upon The Midnight Clear" ...

**Gabriel:** *(interrupts)* "The First Noel" and "Hark! The Herald Angels Sing."

**Michael:** But sadly enough, many of these songs are banned in public schools. Why can't people celebrate the sacred mystery of this holy season for what it is?

*(The accompanist begins to softly play "O Come, All Ye Faithful.")*

**Gabriel:** Listen! I hear music. It's coming from *(name your church)*. Listen.

*(The music gets louder and the audience joins in singing.)*

**Michael:** *(after the hymn)* Nothing's going to stop them from singing or take away their Christmas joy in celebration of the Savior's birth. Come, Gabriel. It's almost Christmas day and we must return to the throne of God. There we will also sing God's praises and worship the Son of God and Savior of the world. He alone is worthy of our highest honor, praise, and glory.

*(Michael and Gabriel begin to exit together, stage left.)*

**Gabriel:** Merry Christmas, Michael.

**Michael:** Merry Christmas to you, Gabriel. And may God bless us all on earth and in heaven.

*(Michael and Gabriel complete their exit.)*

# It's So Christmas-See!

## A One-Act Modern Christmas Drama

## Myra Shofner

# It's So Christmas-See!

**Setting**

It is early evening a few days before Christmas in the living room of Nora Fletcher.

**Production Notes**

The set can be as simple or as detailed as you like. Furnishings should include a sofa, a couple chairs, a desk, a television set, and a Christmas tree.

**Characters**
  Nora
  Carolyn
  First Child
  Second Child
  Tom
  Ralph
  Aunt Ida
  Offstage Voice
  Carolers
  Nativity Scene Persona (optional)

**Sound Effects**
  Sound of carolers in the distance
  Salvation Army bell ringing
  Key turning in the latch
  Telephone ringing
  Doorbell
  Recorded voice of a young woman

**Props**
  Couch or furniture
  Large shopping bag filled with unwrapped presents
  Wrapped presents
  Vacuum cleaner
  Dust cloth, furniture polish, and candles to light (work for Carolyn)
  Candlelighter
  Stacks of Christmas cards, opened and unopened
  Junk mail
  Pen
  Telephone
  Wastebasket
  Bible
  Letter to open and read

Cup of tea
Tape of *The Andy Griffith Show*
Heating pad
Television
Christmas tree
Snow globe
Manger (optional)

---

*(It is evening, a few days before Christmas. As the lights come up on the living room of Nora Fletcher's home, Carolyn is running the vacuum. She turns it off and as she rewinds the cord, in the distance can be heard Christmas carols and the ringing of a Salvation Army bell. A key turns in the lock and Nora Fletcher enters stage left, carrying wrapped packages and a large shopping bag filled with unwrapped presents.)*

**Nora:** *(places her shopping bag and packages on the table with a disgusted grunt)* Yuck! What a rat race!

**Carolyn:** Ma'am?

**Nora:** I said, "What a rat race!" All this Christmas shopping. Every year the stores get more crowded and the associates get more rude! If all the world's a stage, it's time for a new plot! *(wearily rubs the back of her neck)*

**Carolyn:** *(places packages under the tree)* Oh, but didn't you have fun? I love Christmas! There's so much excitement in the air. Shopping and children and music and ... it's all so ... so Christmas-See! *(shakes one of the packages)* Sounds interesting.

**Nora:** *(glances in her direction)* That one's for Bob and Martha Kennedy. She let it drop in Sunday school class that they really need a new toaster. Poor thing. Imagine not being able to afford a toaster. But that man she's married to is a real spendthrift — always buying guns and tools and vintage cars and heaven knows what other things they don't need. He's in over his head! If there was such a thing as debtor's prison, he'd be in it.

**Carolyn:** Well, Mrs. Fletcher, you know how it is. Some people pay their bills when due, some pay when their bills are overdue. He must be one of those who never do. But, it's real sweet of you to get her a toaster! Christmas just makes you want to do nice things, doesn't it?

**Nora:** A guilt trip can make you do the same thing! *(gives her a sarcastic look)* You seem to be a serious-minded woman. I don't know how you can enjoy all of this hullabaloo. I find the season to be a big chore. Crowds pushing and shoving. Children running about — almost knocking you down while parents, obviously out of control, scream at them. Not to mention trying to pick out the right gift for everyone on your Christmas list. Fun? I don't think so.

**Carolyn:** Mrs. Fletcher, it doesn't matter what you give to someone. It's the thought that counts!

**Nora:** Ha, ha, you silly woman! You've met my Aunt Ida. Last year I must have spent three hours worth of thought on the perfect gift for her. And what did that dear lady do? *(mimics)* I'm sorry, Nora, but the color of this shawl will clash terribly with my new winter coat. You won't mind, will you, dear, if we take it back and exchange it? *(changes tone)* I had to spend the entire day after Christmas trotting around with her through all the department stores while she searched for just the right thing!

**Carolyn:** She probably just wanted to spend some time with you.

**Nora:** *(thoughtfully)* I should have given her a gift certificate.

**Carolyn:** Why didn't you?

**Nora:** Because then she would have been upset about my not putting any thought into her gift.

**Carolyn:** Oh, Mrs. Fletcher, I know your aunt loves you. She likes to be with you. This year, instead of shopping for her, why don't you take her out to lunch and give her a promise card?

**Nora:** A promise card? What in the world is a promise card?

**Carolyn:** Children give them to their parents all the time. They take a blank card and write a promise to their parents on it — like "I promise to wash the dishes for a whole week without complaining" or "I promise to keep my room spic and span without being told."

**Nora:** Sweet, but Aunt Ida has a maid to wash her dishes and I already keep my room spic and span.

**Carolyn:** Oh, I didn't mean those exact promises. I meant make her a promise she would appreciate.

**Nora:** And that would be...?

**Carolyn:** Well ... you could promise to spend more time with her or take her to a special place that you both would enjoy — instead of giving her some *thing*.

**Nora:** But then she wouldn't have anything to exchange! *(shakes her head)* I'd better keep looking until I come up with something that is exactly right, something that costs in the neighborhood of what she'll spend on me — which is always more than she should spend! *(pauses)* I'd better get busy wrapping these gifts so that I can deliver them first thing in the morning. After that, I'll hit the mall again and finish up. Who knows, I might just get lucky and find Aunt Ida's perfect gift right off. I'm glad Christmas doesn't come but once a year. The stress is just too much. By the way, I hope you like the gift I got for you. *(telephone rings)* If that's for me, I'm not taking any calls. I can't be civil to another human being today!

**Carolyn:** *(answers telephone)* Hello. Oh, hi, Mrs. Griffin. *(Nora shakes her finger in a "No" gesture and steps out of the room.)* I'm sorry. Mrs. Fletcher can't come to the phone, she's ... she's very busy. Is there something I can help you with? Beauty shop, huh? 9:30 tomorrow morning. Okay, I'll tell her.

**Nora:** *(reenters and hears part of the conversation)* She wants me to drive her to the beauty parlor, doesn't she?

**Carolyn:** Yes.

**Nora:** Well, I'll appreciate it if you will cover for me. I have a million things to do tomorrow. I really don't have time to be Aunt Ida's chauffeur. She has enough money to hire a cab, you know. I mean if you ...

**Carolyn:** *(interrupts)* It's all right. I don't mind. She's really a delightful person.

**Nora:** Aunt Ida? *(gives her a disbelieving look)* You must be some kind of saint! *(crosses to desk and picks up a stack of mail and begins tossing some into the wastebasket while stacking the others)* Getting off the junk mailing list is harder than putting toothpaste back in the tube! *And* look at all these cards I received from people whose names weren't even on my list. Now I'll have to address their cards after dinner and rush them down to the post office first thing tomorrow and hope that they get them in time for Christmas. I'm glad the post office delivers on Christmas day.

**Carolyn:** Don't you love reading your Christmas cards? Along with a cup of hot chocolate? Don't they make you feel so ... so Christmas-See?

**Nora:** Well, I've glanced through mine — they are ... sweet. Some of them are from people I haven't seen since college. Don't know why they keep sending them. I keep hoping they will miss a year so I can stop responding. It's a lot of pressure making sure that I don't leave anyone out. And they keep writing these little notes about their children or their trip to the Grand Canyon. And most of them include some little question that they expect me to answer.

**Carolyn:** They remember you fondly, I'm sure. That's why they are interested in you.

**Nora:** Turn around.

**Carolyn:** Ma'am? *(turns around)*

**Nora:** I don't see them.

**Carolyn:** Them?

**Nora:** Your wings. *(pauses)* Listen, Carolyn, it's enough work just signing my name without jotting down some tidbit about my personal life. Now I've got to get upstairs and wrap these presents.

**Carolyn:** Dinner is ...

**Nora:** I'll grab a bite later. *(Christmas carols are heard in the distance.)* Oh no, it's the church carolers. I had forgotten this was the night for them to come by. They'll expect us to invite them in.

**Carolyn:** Sounds like fun. I'll make some hot chocolate.

**Nora:** Make my excuses instead. If you serve hot chocolate they'll stay forever.

**Carolyn:** But, Mrs. Fletcher, it's Christmas. You don't want to miss ...

**Nora:** *(interrupts)* I really am not in the mood for singing. I need to wrap these presents. And, remember, don't appreciate the carolers too much. Let them sing a couple of songs and then be on their way. *(nods in the direction of the desk)* Don't forget I've still got that stack of cards to address! *(exits)*

*(Carolyn opens the door and welcomes the carolers inside. This can be staged as simply or as detailed as desired. The carolers may enter loudly chattering to one another and take their places about the room while the pianist plays lively music or the carolers may be spotlighted as they sing. They may exit chattering or simply kill the spotlight. As they leave, the telephone rings.)*

**Carolyn:** *(answers telephone)* Hello. Reverend Blackwell, how are you? Fine. Oh, I ... she's .... busy right now. May I take a message? *(listens)* Oh, that's too bad. I hope she will be better soon. *(listens)* I'll tell Mrs. Fletcher. *(listens)* Well, it may be in the morning before she can call you back ... *(listens)* Yes, sir, I'll tell her you said it is very important. Good night, Reverend Blackwell.

**Nora:** *(enters)* And what did the good pastor want this time? I've already written my check for the mission offering and sent my food for the Christmas baskets. Not to mention the check I sent to the homeless shelter. It was more than generous this year.

**Carolyn:** *(hesitantly)* Well ...

**Nora:** Oh, no. He's asked something unpleasant of me, hasn't he?

**Carolyn:** He said Mrs. Wanaker has pneumonia.

**Nora:** *(relieved)* Oh. Well, call Charley's takeout and order some of his won-ton soup sent over. And tell Charley to put in some tuna for Bessie Mae's old cat. She'll be more worried about Tabby than about herself. Of course, Tabby is the best family member she's got. That good-for-nothing son of hers stays too deep in trouble to take care of her. She says he's trying to mend his ways, but if you ask me, he must be using weak thread. Now, I'd better tackle those Christmas cards.

**Carolyn:** *(speaks quickly)* She isn't going to be able to have the children from the children's home like she planned.

**Nora:** I should hope not. She's in no condition to care for children.

**Carolyn:** The pastor wants you to take them.

**Nora:** What?

**Carolyn:** He says there is no one else. Everyone else has already signed up for children.

**Nora:** I can't do something like that on such short notice. That would mean more shopping and planning.

**Carolyn:** I told him you would call him in the morning.

**Nora:** I certainly will. He should know better than to expect me to step in last minute. Tom and I always invited two or three of them for Christmas, but this year I don't have time to be bothered. They're a lot of work, you know.

**Carolyn:** Mrs. Fletcher, I don't mean to ... I mean, it's probably none of my business ... but I can help you care for them.

**Nora:** I knew it! You are an angel! Where'd you hang your halo? *(pauses)* But even with your help, I can't possibly do it. This year I am simply too busy.

**Carolyn:** But having children in the house at Christmas would be so ...

**Nora:** *(interrupts)* Christmas-See!

**Carolyn:** If you don't take the children, aren't you afraid you might be missing ... you know, missing something wonderful? Maybe missing Christmas without realizing it?

**Nora:** *(gives her a look)* Missing Christmas? Carolyn, I am experiencing Christmas in all its glory — grumpy salespeople, crowded stores, endless commercials pushing products no one needs, solicitations of funds from every charity known to mankind, not to mention having to sit through the *Nutcracker* for the umpteenth time! To tell the truth, I think the season has become Chris-*messy*. Now, if you will excuse me, I need to address those cards.

*(Carolyn exits. Nora sits at the desk and begins to address the cards, then throws the pen down angrily.)*

**Nora:** Missing Christmas? Why did she say that? Just to make me feel guilty? About Aunt Ida — the carolers — the children? Well, I refuse to feel guilty. I'm doing the best I can. Besides — what if I do "miss Christmas" this year? What would be so bad about that? Christmas is supposed to be a happy time. 'Tis the season to be jolly! Instead, everyone acts like they have a chip on their shoulders. No matter what you do for them or give them, it never seems to be enough. Christmas can't seem to live up to anybody's expectations! All the hustle and bustle in the department stores is just a phony facade, a created excuse for boosting sales, a reason for people to get what they want! I'm sick of it! Sick of it all! Why does there have to be a Christmas? I certainly wouldn't miss it! Without Christmas, I wouldn't have to run all over town tomorrow delivering presents that won't fit people who don't like the color anyway. I can just sit in my easy chair, put my feet up, and watch reruns of *The Andy Griffith Show*. (*Goes over to her chair, sits down, and turns the television on. Sleepily, her head begins to nod.* The Andy Griffith Show *noise diminishes.*)

(*Two children and a young father enter and seat themselves on the couch. Or, this scene may be played in the spotlight.*)

**First Child:** (*claps hands in delight*) Oh, the tree is so beautiful. I love the angel on top. And I love the presents under the tree. Why do we get presents on Christmas, Daddy? It's not our birthday!

**Second Child:** Because we have been very good children.

**Tom:** Is that what you think? Well, you are good children. But that's not the reason we give you presents at Christmas. Let's read the Christmas story from the Bible. Maybe you can figure out the reason for yourself. (*opens the Bible and reads the Christmas story*)

**First Child:** That was nice of the kings to bring those presents, wasn't it, Daddy?

**Tom:** Yes, it was.

**First Child:** My friend, Sarah, told me that Jesus was a birthday present.

**Second Child:** No. Jesus *got* birthday presents — from the kings.

**First Child:** Sarah said Jesus was a birthday present because God so loved the world that he gave his only begotten Son. When you give something, it is a present. (*smiles*) Sarah said God gave us Jesus and Mary wrapped him up!

**Second Child:** She did not!

**First Child:** That's what the Bible says! Mary wrapped him in swaddling clothes and laid him in a manger.

**Second Child:** Oh.

**Tom:** So, why do we give presents at Christmas?

**First Child:** Everybody should get presents on their birthday. But we can't bring Jesus presents like the wise men did, so we give them to others. Because we love the world just like God!

**Second Child:** Will I still get presents even if I am not very good?

**Tom:** That sounds like a question for another time. Let's get you two tucked in. You need to get some sleep. Tomorrow will be an exciting day! *(exits with the children or simply kill the spotlight)*

*(Sounds from the television increase and waken Nora. She shudders, turns off the television, and is surprised to find Carolyn standing beside her.)*

**Carolyn:** Oh, I'm sorry. I didn't mean to startle you. You must have been having a pleasant dream.

**Nora:** Why?

**Carolyn:** You were smiling.

**Nora:** *(softly and thoughtfully)* I was dreaming about Tom and the children ... at Christmas ... *(tone changes abruptly)* Did you need something? *(nods in the direction of the desk)* I really must finish those cards.

**Carolyn:** I'm sorry, but someone is at the door. He wants to see you — personally.

**Nora:** Oh, Carolyn. No! Take care of it.

**Carolyn:** I tried, but he insisted. I really think you should talk to him. He has something very special to tell you. I'm sure he won't take too much time.

**Nora:** *(heaves a sigh)* Okay. Bring him in.

*(Carolyn exits and returns with a man who is warmly, but poorly, dressed. Nora looks puzzled. The man offers his hand.)*

**Ralph:** Mrs. Fletcher, it is good to meet you. My name is Ralph Peterson.

**Nora:** Please, sit down.

**Ralph:** Oh no, ma'am. I won't be but a minute. It's Christmas *(nods at Carolyn)* she told me you are very busy.

**Nora:** Well ...

**Ralph:** *(interrupts)* I came to thank you, Mrs. Fletcher.

**Nora:** To thank me?

**Ralph:** Yes, ma'am. To thank you for what you did for my family.

**Nora:** I don't understand. What exactly have I done for your family?

**Ralph:** I don't want to get in any trouble, but ... We found out by mistake. Joey, that's my son, saw it on Dr. Palmer's desk by accident.

**Nora:** Dr. Palmer?

**Ralph:** The director of the homeless shelter.

**Nora:** Oh ... yes. Saw what?

**Ralph:** Your check.

**Nora:** My check?

**Ralph:** Yes, ma'am. Earlier this week, Joey, my wife, and I ended up at the homeless shelter. We've been living in our car ever since I lost my job. But it's getting too cold to stay there anymore and Joey, well, Joey has been real sick. So we decided we'd better get ourselves inside and try to find some help for Joey.

**Nora:** So you went to the homeless shelter?

**Ralph:** Yes, ma'am. Well, Dr. Palmer was really nice and when we told him our story, he smiled and said something like, "The Lord Jesus sure has good timing, doesn't he?" Then he said he had just received a very generous Christmas check from a woman who had marked, "for someone with a special need" on the envelope. He said he figured our showing up meant the check was for us.

**Nora:** We always send a check at Christmas. At least, Tom *did*, now I do.

**Ralph:** Dr. Palmer sent us to a doctor to see about Joey and when we got back he fed us a good, warm meal and put us up for the night.

**Nora:** As well he should!

**Ralph:** This morning, Dr. Palmer gave me a suit and money for a haircut and a list of people to see about a job. Well, ma'am, a man hired me! I have a job.

**Nora:** That's good news. And your son, Joey?

**Ralph:** Oh, ma'am, the medicine fixed Joey up real good. He's going to be fine. We could never have afforded that doctor, Mrs. Fletcher, without your help.

**Nora:** That's why Tom ...

**Ralph:** *(interrupts)* So this afternoon when Joey told us that he had accidentally seen your name and address on that check — Joey's a smart boy, ma'am, got a memory like a steel trap — I knew I had to come here and thank you personally.

**Nora:** That's kind of you, but ...

**Ralph:** Well, I won't take up anymore of your time. I know how busy you are. But God bless you, ma'am. We won't ever forget you. Thank you for sharing the Christmas spirit with us.

**Nora:** The Christmas spirit? Well ... I ... I mean, I ...

**Ralph:** My wife and I decided that when we get back on our feet, the first thing we are going to do is write a check to that homeless shelter — in your name, Mrs. Fletcher — you know, just to keep the Christmas spirit going. You don't mind, do you?

**Nora:** *(astounded, almost speechless)* No, but ...

**Ralph:** *(extends his hand)* I'm going to get out of here and let you get busy with ... well, with all the things you need to do. *(smiles)* Dr. Palmer told us to use some of the money to buy Christmas presents for Joey ... well, we've got to wrap 'em up, you know. *(shakes hands with Nora)* Thanks again, ma'am, for having Christmas in your heart.

**Nora:** *(slightly shaken)* You're welcome. *(watches the door as Ralph exits; doesn't see Carolyn enter and stand close behind her)*

**Carolyn:** *(holds a cup of tea)* I thought you might feel ...

**Nora:** *(continues to stare in the direction of the door)* Christmas-See?

**Carolyn:** Like having a cup of tea.

**Nora:** *(turns around)* That was some experience!

**Carolyn:** What experience, Mrs. Fletcher?

**Nora:** *(takes the cup of tea)* The visit with Ralph.

**Carolyn:** Ralph? Ralph who, Mrs. Fletcher?

**Nora:** *(looks at her quizzically)* The man who just ... you let him in ...

**Carolyn:** *(interrupts)* Pardon me, ma'am, but I've been in the kitchen — making tea.

**Nora:** *(recovers, but is obviously confused)* I ... I must have been mistaken. Thanks for the tea, Carolyn. *(begins to drink as Carolyn exits; the telephone rings, she sets the cup down and answers it)* Hello. Oh, hi, Aunt Ida. *(slightly irritably)* I'm very well, thank you, just terribly busy. It is Christmas. How are you? *(pauses)* Oh, I'm sorry — rheumatism? *(pauses)* It is? On the blink, huh? Well, why don't I send Carolyn over with *our* heating pad? *(pauses)* You are? Are you sure you feel up to coming over here? *(pauses)* You are? Yes, Aunt Ida, cell phones are a modern marvel. *(knock at the door)* You're kidding?

*(Nora places the telephone in its cradle and goes to answer the door. While she does this, Carolyn enters and places the heating pad on a nearby chair. Aunt Ida enters.)*

**Aunt Ida:** *(looks around the room and her eyes light on the tree)* Your tree is magnificent, Nora! But then, it always is. *(surveys the room)* I remember so many parties here when this room rang with the sounds of Christmas.

**Nora:** *(turns away and speaks, almost to herself)* That was a long time ago, Aunt Ida. Tom was still alive and he loved ... I'm weary of Christmas ... *(to Aunt Ida)* Sorry about your rheumatism.

**Aunt Ida:** Thank you. It's poor company, but I can live with it! It's just that a heating pad does help. When I discovered that mine wasn't working, I thought I'd pop over and borrow yours. I called a cab and here I am. *(pauses)* Actually, Nora, I really wanted to see you ... to talk to you. I have something very important to say.

**Nora:** Oh? *(indicates that they be seated)* Would you like some tea? Carolyn can ...

**Aunt Ida:** *(interrupts, confused with a questioning look)* Carolyn? *(without waiting for an answer)* No, no tea, thank you. I can't stay very long. *(both sit)* My Sunday school class is coming over this evening for our Christmas party. Everything's ready. The girls will bring covered dishes so there really wasn't that much for me to do. *(sighs)* Dear me, the holidays are a busy time, aren't they? It seems like I have been running the entire Christmas season. So many parties and friends dropping by. And, of course, all of the children have picked me up and carted me all over the place — not to mention the programs at church.

**Nora:** Oh? It must be very tiring for ...

**Aunt Ida:** *(interrupts)* I love it! It keeps me young. *(looks at Nora)* But, I'm sorry we haven't been able to get together. That's why I wanted you to drive me to the beauty shop. I needed to drop off Maggie's present. Then I thought the two of us would have a nice lunch together — my treat. I'm sorry you are too busy. I decided I'd better run over here so we can talk.

**Nora:** *(puzzled)* Talk?

**Aunt Ida:** I know how lonely you must be with the children studying in Europe and Tom gone.

**Nora:** Me? Lonely? Aunt Ida, I don't have time to be lonely! I am perfectly fine.

**Aunt Ida:** Oh, well ... *(obviously not convinced)* I'm glad to hear that, Nora. That's ... good.

**Nora:** And we will get together, Aunt Ida, after the madness of the holidays. I promise. Let's just get through Christmas first.

**Aunt Ida:** *(stands)* Well, if you are sure.

**Nora:** *(stands and gets the heating pad)* I'm sure. *(hands heating pad to Aunt Nora and kisses her on the cheek)* Do you need a ride home? I can have Carolyn ...

**Aunt Ida:** Oh, honey, no. Max, my friend from church, drives the cab. He's waiting for me. *(winks)* He gives me a special rate.

**Nora:** Aunt Ida!

**Aunt Ida:** Oh, don't worry, Nora. He's bald as an Easter egg. Doesn't bother him, though. He says God only covers up the heads he doesn't like. Besides, he's old enough to be ... *(chuckles)* Well, maybe you ought to worry — just a little.

*(Aunt Nora exits left as Carolyn enters right.)*

**Nora:** That's a twist. Aunt Ida wants to hang out with me because *she* thinks I'm lonely.

**Carolyn:** Ma'am?

**Nora:** Nothing. I was muttering to myself. *(looks in the direction of the desk, shakes her head, crosses, sits, and begins again to address envelopes)*

**Carolyn:** *(reaches down and picks up a card from the floor)* Did you drop this one, Mrs. Fletcher?

**Nora:** *(looks more closely at the card as Carolyn slips out of the room)* I don't think so. This one wasn't in the stack. I have looked through the cards twice, Carolyn. *(turns toward where Carolyn had been standing)* Carolyn? Now where did she go? I'm beginning to think she is some kind of apparition. The way she comes and goes — it's like she can walk through walls. *(looks at the card again)* Elizabeth Martin? *(opens the card and reads to herself)*

**Offstage Voice:** Dear Mrs. Fletcher, can you believe I have been in Hot Springs for three years? Well, this year something wonderful has happened. I met a wonderful Christian man at our church, and we have fallen in love. We are going to be married on March 2. I wish you could come for the wedding — to share in my joy. It was you, after all, who helped me get my life straightened out and made this day a possibility.

**Nora:** Elizabeth Martin — such a scared young thing — being arrested for writing bad checks three days before Christmas. Tom and I discovered her when we did our jail ministry visitation. Tom talked the judge into letting her come home with us. When we put her on that bus back to her parents' home, she was so afraid! Sounds like things have turned out pretty well for her. *(continues reading the letter)*

**Offstage Voice:** But most of all, I want to thank you and your husband for telling me about Jesus and how to be saved. It took a while for it to sink in, but I want you to know that I gave my heart to

Jesus a few weeks ago. This will be my first real Christmas because this year I will have Christmas in my heart. Thank you forever, and Merry Christmas. Love, Elizabeth.

**Nora:** *(folds the card and places it into its envelope as Carolyn enters with a present and extends it to Nora)* For me? *(Carolyn nods; Nora opens the present and takes out a snow globe)* It's the Nativity. How beautiful. Who is it from? *(searches for a card)* There's no card.

*(Nora shakes the snow globe. The spotlight is on the manger scene. This can be staged as simply or as detailed as the director wishes it to be.)*

**Nora:** Oh, I had almost forgotten how beautiful the story of Christmas is. And what Christmas truly means. *(with conviction)* Aunt Ida is right. I am lonely. Since Tom died, I've been closing my heart to everyone around me; shutting them out of my life. I have been such a fool! I nearly missed Christmas this year! *(looks upward)* Dear Lord, thank you for reminding me that Christmas must live in my heart. *(looks around and calls with enthusiasm)* Carolyn ... *(bewildered)* Now where did she vanish this time? *(steps toward stage right and calls again)* Carolyn? *(telephone rings and Nora answers it)*

Hello. Oh, hello, Aunt Ida. *(doorbell rings, Nora cups her hand over the receiver and calls)* Carolyn? *(speaks into the receiver)* I'm sorry, Aunt Ida, but my doorbell is ringing and Carolyn isn't answering. *(listens)* Carolyn. My maid, of course ... *(listens)* When did I get a maid? *(surprised)* Why ... you're right — I don't have a maid. Yes, I know I said it, but ... well, Aunt Ida, let's just say that I have had a most unusual evening and leave it at that. *(doorbell rings again)*

Yes, I do need to get the door, but before I hang up, Aunt Ida, I was wondering if you could drop by Christmas Eve? *(listens)* Yes, I'm serious. I would love to spend some time with my favorite aunt. *(listens)* Of course, bring your taxi driver friend. *(doorbell rings again)* Aunt Ida, will you call Reverend Blackwell for me? *(listens)* Tell him I'll be glad to take the children from the orphanage for Christmas. Get the details and call me back. *(listens)*

Huh? Yes, I remember Tom's nurse. I'll never forget her. She took such good care of Tom ... and of me. She was truly an ... angel. *(listens)* Yes, yes, her name was Carolyn.

*(Nora looks in the direction of the manger scene. The angel, Carolyn, enters and takes her place in the scene, adjusting her halo as she slips into place. She smiles and winks at Nora. Nora returns the smile as the doorbell rings again.)*

**Nora:** I'll see you tomorrow night, Aunt Ida. *(hangs up the telephone)*

*(Nora steps to the door to welcome the chattering carolers. As they sing, the other members of the cast enter and take their places about the room. As the song ends, Nora speaks.)*

**Nora:** Now this is what I call Christmas-See....

*(Singing resumes as the play ends.)*

The End

# The Legend Of The North Star

## (Little Dot Makes A Wish)

A Christmas Story
For Children

# Donna J. Fetzer

*I dedicate this story and play
to all my grandchildren and step-grandchildren.
They are the reason I write.*

# Introduction

This story is written in two forms. The first is a story to be read or told to Sunday school classes or at church events such as banquets or Christmas programs.

The second form is a play that is perfect for Christmas. All ages can participate in the production for an outreach event.

# The Legend Of The North Star
## (Little Dot Makes A Wish)

*In the beginning God created day and night, light and darkness, and created the stars that shine like diamonds.*

Many, many years ago, stars were placed in the dark skies to light up the night. One, lone, tiny black dot was left behind. The lonely little dot rolled and darted here and there, around thousands and thousands of glowing points of light.

The little dot heard the names of Orion, Sirius, and Aquarius, but he never heard his name. "What's my name?" he asked all the bigger stars. Many of the stars winked and blinked and slipped away.

One day, stars in the galaxy called the Milky Way gave the tiny dot a name. They called him Little Dot. "Thank you, thank you," he said. Then he asked the stars, "Why don't I glow ... Why am I not big and bright? I just want to be as shiny as the other stars."

One of the largest stars in the Milky Way said, "Don't worry, Little Dot. One day you will be big and you will shine brightly."

"Today would be a good day," Little Dot said. "I could shine and glow and be seen by everyone. Oh, how I wish I could be like the other stars."

Luminaria, wisest of all stars, heard Little Dot. She glided close to him. "I'm giving you one wish," she said. "You must use it wisely, and only when you really need it ... not before," she warned. "Do you think you can do that?"

Little Dot was so excited he did a double roll. "Yes, I can do that!" he answered. "But I already know what my wish is ... I'd like to be the most brilliant star ever."

Sounds of Luminaria's laughter filled the night stars. Glitter flew all about. "That's a very good dream, Little Dot," she said. "But you must remember not to use your wish foolishly." Then in a twinkling of a star, she was gone.

Little Dot thought and thought. "How will I use my wish? Maybe I could become a *rock and roll star*. That would be awesome." He began to play an air guitar, rocking to music only he could hear. "Nooo, that might be considered foolish." He rolled around in the sky thinking, "I know. I could blink on and off at will, fooling all the people below." That made him chuckle. "Wait, I've got it ... I could wish to be a comet with a long, trailing tail of light. That would be beautiful." Little Dot closed his eyes, dreaming. "Maybe I could be a meteor — a shooting star. People on earth believe that if you see a shooting star and make a wish, it will come true." He opened his eyes. "That won't work. How would I get back up in the sky if I fell to Earth? Oh, thinking is such hard work."

Then one night when Little Dot was busy thinking and thinking, he heard the tinkling voices of all the stars. Something was happening down on Earth. Little Dot flew through the clouds, searching for Luminaria. "What's going on?" he asked. "Everyone sounds so excited, and I don't know what's happening."

"Let me tell you," Luminaria whispered. "Look closely, and listen carefully. Can you see the fields outside the town of Bethlehem?"

Little Dot peeked through the clouds. "Yes, I do."

"Can you see the shepherds watching over their flocks of sheep?"
"Yes, yes! I do."
"Do you see how light the dark sky is becoming?"
"It is lighter! I see the shepherds looking up in the sky!" he said. "Can they see me?"
"No, Little Dot, they can't see you, but they can see the angel."
"I see the angel, too!" he shouted. "The shepherds look afraid. What's the matter?"
"Shhhhh, listen, Little Dot," Luminaria said, "the angel is speaking."

*I am bringing you news of great joy. Tonight in the city of Bethlehem, a Savior has been born. He is called Jesus Christ and he is our Lord.*

Luminaria whispered in Little Dot's ear. "That's why all the stars are excited. The angel is looking for a special star to lead three wise men from the Far East, who have been watching the night skies for many years. They believe that some day a new star will rise to announce the birth of their king."

Little Dot nearly rolled out of the sky. "A new star! I could be that star! I wish to be the brightest, the most brilliant and shiny star in the sky." Luminaria glistened brightly and nodded.

Three wise men were riding on their camels bearing gifts for the Christ Child. They saw the brightest star they had ever seen in the night sky. They followed the light of that brilliant star to Bethlehem. The star stopped above the stable where Jesus lay in a manger — fulfilling God's plan. The three wise men raised their gifts high over their heads in thanks.

Little Dot got his wish. He *was* that shining star, and he was given his true name — the Star of Bethlehem.

The End

# The Legend Of The North Star

## (Little Dot Makes A Wish)

A Christmas Play
For Youth Of All Ages

# Donna J. Fetzer

# The Legend Of The North Star
## (Little Dot Makes A Wish)

**Summary**

A storyteller tells the "Legend Of The North Star," a story about Little Dot, who was left behind in the night sky after all the stars had been created. Little Dot is curious as to why he doesn't have a name, and why he doesn't look like the other stars in the sky. Luminaria, the wisest of all stars, heard Little Dot make a wish to be like the other stars. She grants him one wish. After Little Dot thinks of several humorous ways to use his wish, Luminaria returns and helps him discover his real name and his purpose. He becomes the Star of Bethlehem.

**Characters**
- Storyteller
- Luminaria — wisest of all stars, gives Little Dot a wish he must use wisely
- Little Dot — left behind after God created the stars
- Orion, Sirius, Aquarius — stars
- Milky Way — a galaxy of stars (several children can be the galaxy)
- Angel
- Joseph (nonspeaking)
- Mary (nonspeaking)
- Three Wise Men (nonspeaking)
- Shepherds — two or three (nonspeaking)
- Little Stars and Clouds (nonspeaking)
- Choir — adult and/or junior (nonspeaking)

**Props**
- Two high stools draped with white netting and tinsel (to look like clouds)
- One low stool (decorated as above)
- Chair (decorated as above)
- Two or three low palm trees
- Cardboard sheep
- Shepherds' staffs with cardboard sheep attached
- Staff
- Baby Jesus (doll wrapped in white cloth)
- Manger
- Lightweight silver pole with brilliant star attached
- Battery-operated blinking Christmas lights (one for each star)
- Gifts
- Large book
- Pouches to hold tinsel
- Tiny bells
- Pen lights, battery-operated candles, or flashlights (optional)

**Costumes**

    Storyteller — white flowing robe, a shiny headdress, ballerina slippers
    Little Stars — white robes with tinsel streamers, blinking star headdresses, white ballerina slippers
    Choir — white, flowing robes, blinking star headdresses, white ballerina slippers, pouches of Christmas tinsel
    Joseph and Shepherds — robes, head scarves, staffs, sandals
    Mary — long, blue dress, head scarf, shawl, sandals, carrying doll
    Little Dot — all in black — black slippers (no flip-flops or sandals); later all in silver
    Luminaria — silvery, flowing gown with lots of tinsel attached, bright blinking star headdress, white ballerina slippers, pouch of tinsel
    Clouds — white netting and tinsel made into fluffy clouds, white tights, fluffy headdress, white ballerina slippers, pouches of tinsel
    Angel — long, flowing dress, wings, halo with tinsel streamers, white ballerina slippers

**Setting**

The play takes place in the sky before Christmas Eve. The lights are low. The backdrop is painted dark with twinkling stars (blinking Christmas lights) and white clouds made from white netting and Christmas tinsel. The stage should have three levels: a platform, risers, and lower stage area. The choir will be on the risers, each dressed in white with a star headdress. There will be actors dressed as stars and clouds on the platform in the background. The set should give the illusion of being in the sky.

On the platform is one cloud chair stage right, two high cloud stools, and one low cloud stool stage left. On the lower level of stage left are two or three low palm trees and sheep. Storyteller has a large book she reads from. Offstage right is a manger to be brought center stage as the choir sings. Mary and Joseph enter at that time.

---

*(It is night. The stars are twinkling. Children dressed as stars and clouds are in the background. The choir is standing on the risers. Storyteller enters stage right carrying a large book. She sits on the cloud chair, opens the book, and motions for Little Stars to come.)*

**Storyteller:** Come, my twinkling little stars and I will tell you about the legend of the North Star. *(Little Stars gather around the Storyteller to hear the legend)* In the beginning God created day and night, light and darkness, and created the stars that shine like diamonds. Many years ago, stars were placed in the dark skies to light up the night. One lone, tiny black dot was left behind after the stars were placed in the sky. The lonely little dot rolled and darted here and there, around thousands and thousands of glowing points of light.

*(Little Stars stand, face the audience, put their arms around each other, rocking back and forth as they sing, "Twinkle, Twinkle, Little Star." Little Dot, doing a cartwheel enters stage left and stops center stage. Orion, Sirius, Aquarius enter stage right from the background scene and float around Little Dot.)*

**Orion, Sirius, Aquarius:** *(playfully)* Hi, I'm Orion. This is Sirius and Aquarius. We're important stars. Who ... are you?

**Little Dot:** *(looks unhappy)* I'm, I'm ... I don't know. I'm just a dot in the night sky. I don't have a name.

**Orion, Sirius, Aquarius:** That's too bad ... maybe some day ...

*(Waving, Orion, Sirius, and Aquarius join the stars in the background. Little Dot floats over to other stars.)*

**Storyteller:** The little dot wanted a name. He asked all the bigger stars if they knew his name. They just blinked and winked and slipped away. The stars didn't have an answer.

*(Milky Way, a galaxy of several stars, enters together from the background scene.)*

**Storyteller:** One day, a galaxy called the Milky Way, floated beside the little dot.

*(Milky Way floats to Little Dot.)*

**Milky Way:** *(only one star speaks)* I know you would like a name. We heard it from the star-line, and we have just the perfect name for you. *(Other Milky Way stars nod and agree)* Yes, yes, the perfect name.

**Little Dot:** *(uncertain)* Really?

**Milky Way:** You will be called Little Dot.

**Little Dot:** *(excitedly)* Thank you, thank you. I love my name. *(downcast)* But ... why don't I glow like the other stars? Why am I not big and bright? I just want to be as shiny as the other stars.

**Milky Way:** *(only one star speaks)* Don't worry, Little Dot. One day you will be big, and you will shine brightly. *(all start to leave)*

**Little Dot:** *(enthusiastically)* Wait ... today would be a good day. I could shine and glow and be seen by everyone.

*(Milky Way stars giggle, tiny bells ring as they exit.)*

**Little Dot:** *(sighs)* Oh, how I wish I could be like the other stars. *(sits down on the cloud stool)*

**Storyteller:** Luminaria, wisest of all stars, heard Little Dot make that wish.

*(Luminaria enters stage right. She floats close to Little Dot.)*

**Luminaria:** Hello, Little Dot. I am Luminaria, the wisest of all stars. I heard you make a wish.

**Little Dot:** *(surprised, jumps up)* Luminaria!

**Luminaria:** *(smiles)* Yes, and I am going to grant you one wish ... only one. You must use it wisely, and only when you really need it ... and not before. Do you think you can do that?

**Little Dot:** *(excitedly)* Yes, yes, I can do that! But I already know what my wish is ... I'd like to be the most brilliant star ever.

**Luminaria:** *(motherly)* That's a very good dream, Little Dot. But you must remember not to use your wish foolishly.

*(Tiny bells ring and tinsel falls from above as Luminaria exits.)*

**Storyteller:** Well, Little Dot was very excited. He began thinking and thinking how he might use that one and only wish.

**Little Dot:** *(thinking, he strolls back and forth)* How will I use my wish? *(stops walking)*
  Maybe ... I could become a rock and roll star. Yesss! *(begins playing an air guitar and dancing to music only he can hear, then stops playing)* Nooo, that might be considered foolish. *(sits down, thinks, jumps up)*
  I know, I could blink on and off at will, fooling all the people below. *(chuckles)*
  Wait, I've got it ... I could wish to be a, uh, comet, with a long trailing tail of light *(motions a long tail of light behind him, then nods and sits down)* Yes, yes ... that would be beautiful. *(closes his eyes and dreams)*
  Or, maybe a meteor ... a shooting star. People on earth believe that if you see a shooting star and make a wish, it will come true. *(opens his eyes and jumps up)* That won't work. How would I get back up in the sky if I fell to Earth? *(sits down on the cloud stool in the position of The Thinker)* Oh, thinking is such hard work.

**Storyteller:** Then one night, when Little Dot was busy thinking and thinking, he heard the tinkling voices of all the stars.

*(Tiny little bells ring. Little Dot stands up and looks up, down, and all around.)*

**Storyteller:** Something was happening down on Earth. Little Dot flew through clouds, searching for Luminaria.

*(Little Dot floats around the Stars and Clouds looking for Luminaria.)*

**Little Dot:** Luminaria, Luminaria, where are you?

*(Luminaria enters as the tinkling bells continue to ring softly.)*

**Luminaria:** *(reassuringly)* I'm right here, Little Dot. Come and sit with me.

**Little Dot:** *(worried)* What's going on? Everyone sounds so excited, and I don't know what's happening.

*(Little Dot and Luminaria sit on the two high stools, and look below. Choir sings "O Little Town Of Bethlehem." Shepherds enter from stage left, carrying staffs with sheep attached. One stands, one sits beside the palm trees.)*

**Luminaria:** *(when the Choir stops, whispers)* Let me tell you, Little Dot, what is happening. Look closely, and listen carefully. *(points)* Can you see the fields outside the town of Bethlehem?

**Little Dot:** Yes, I do.

**Luminaria:** Can you see the shepherds watching over their flocks of sheep?

**Little Dot:** Yes, yes, I do!

**Luminaria:** Do you see how light the dark sky is becoming?

*(Lights are slowly turned up.)*

**Little Dot:** *(amazed)* It is lighter! I see the shepherds looking up in the sky! Can they see me?

**Luminaria:** No, Little Dot, they can't see you, but they can see the angel below.

*(Choir sings verse 1 of "While Shepherds Watched Their Flocks By Night." The Angel appears and stands on the risers above the Shepherds. The Shepherds look up and appear to be frightened.)*

**Little Dot:** *(loudly)* I see the angel, too. The shepherds look afraid. What's the matter?

**Luminaria:** *(whispers)* Shhhh, listen, Little Dot. The angel is speaking.

**Angel:** I am bringing you news of great joy. Tonight in the city of Bethlehem, a Savior has been born. He is called Jesus Christ and he is our Lord.

*(Choir sings verses 2 and 3 of "While Shepherds Watched Their Flocks By Night." The manger is moved to center stage.)*

**Luminaria:** *(whispers)* That's why all the stars are excited. The angel is looking for a special star to lead the three wise men from the Far East, who have been watching the night skies for many years. They believe that some day a new star will rise to announce the birth of their king.

**Little Dot:** *(stands, does two cartwheels, then sits back down)* Wow! They are looking for a new star.

**Luminaria:** *(laughs; tiny bells ring)* Yes, that is true.

**Little Dot:** *(elatedly)* A new star! I could be that star! *(stands, arms outstretched, and looks up)* I wish to be the brightest, the most brilliant and shiny star in the sky.

**Luminaria:** *(nods and smiles)* Wish granted.

*(Luminaria and Little Dot exit. Many tiny bells ring and lots of tinsel falls from above. Little Stars and Clouds sing "Away In The Manger." Mary and Joseph enter stage right. Mary sits beside the manger, holding a baby. Joseph stands beside her. Shepherds carry their staffs with sheep attached, and stand on either side of Mary and Joseph. Little Dot enters stage left on the risers and waits until the singing stops. He is now dressed in silver, carrying a silver pole with a bright, twinkling star attached. Choir sings "We Three Kings." Little Dot walks slowly to center stage and holds the star over the stable scene. Three Wise Men, carrying their gifts, enter from the back and walk slowly down the center aisle as Choir sings. They pause partway and point to the star. They continue to the stage and kneel in front of Mary and Joseph. The singing stops.)*

**Storyteller:** Three wise men were riding on their camels, bearing gifts for the Christ Child. They saw the brightest star they had ever seen in the night sky. They followed the light of that brilliant star to Bethlehem. The star stopped above the stable where Jesus lay in a manger, fulfilling God's plan.

*(Choir sings "What Child Is This?")*

**Storyteller:** Little Dot got his wish. He was that shining star ...

*(Storyteller and Little Stars stand facing the audience, stretch out their arms and look up.)*

**Storyteller:** He was given his true name ... the Star of Bethlehem.

*(With bells ringing and tinsel falling from above, Little Stars hold hands and skip in a circle around Storyteller. They skip left, skip right, and end by kneeling with their hands in prayer position, looking up at Little Dot.)*

*(Audience and all actors sing "Go Tell It On The Mountain.")*

The End

# The Fourth Wise Man

An Epiphany Drama
For Adults Or Older Youth

## Adalya Hadar

# The Fourth Wise Man

**Characters**
    Matthew — gospel writer
    Matthias — son of the fourth wise man
    Wise Man 1
    Wise Man 2
    Wise Man 3
    Wise Man 4

**Props**
    Pen/paper for Matthew
    Small bag for Wise Man 3
    Jar for Wise Man 2
    Box for Wise Man 4
    Gift for Wise Man 1
    Three duffel bags for Wise Men 1, 2, 3
    Candle for Matthew's table
    Two stage blocks for Wise Men
    Table
    Two chairs

**Settings**
    Local gathering place (table, two chairs)
    The road to Bethlehem
    The house in Bethlehem
    The road home for the Wise Men

---

*(The stage should be set with Matthew and Matthias at a table, stage right; the four Wise Men should be set, stage left, with Wise Man 1, Wise Man 2, Wise Man 3 sitting in a loose semicircle, while Wise Man 4 is standing downstage and stage right of them — all Wise Men are frozen in place. Lights come up stage right.)*

**Matthew:** So you're sure that's how it happened?

**Matthias:** Absolutely. No question. *(points to Matthew's paper)* It's in there.

**Matthew:** *(looks at paper as if reviewing notes)* Okay, well, let me make sure I have this all down correctly. These men — these wise men — traveled from the East because they saw a star.

**Matthias:** Not just "a star" — *his* star.

**Matthew:** Right. *His* star. And they went to Jerusalem to see Herod.

**Matthias:** Yes.

**Matthew:** And they told Herod they wanted to worship the new king of the Jews.

**Matthias:** That's right.

**Matthew:** *(looks at Matthias)* And you received this information from whom?

**Matthias:** My father — a most reliable source, I can assure you. He was there. He saw it all.

**Matthew:** Your father. I understand that he recently died.

**Matthias:** Yes *(leans forward in chair)*, but he wanted to make sure that his story was told, so he passed on to me the events surrounding his first trip to Jerusalem.

**Matthew:** And you're certain you've told me *exactly* what he said?

**Matthias:** Word for word.

**Matthew:** Okay, well, there's just one slight problem. You see, I actually met your father and I — well, you know — I just — there's no easy way to say this, but — your father doesn't speak.

**Matthias:** *(sits back and scratches his head)* Oh ... uh, he must have just been having an off day.

**Matthew:** I interviewed him several days in a row. Every day it was the same. Silence except for one word. That's all I could ever get out of him.

**Matthias:** Ah.

**Matthew:** So, who *really* told you the story?

**Matthias:** *(pauses, looks away, and sighs)* My mother.

**Matthew:** And how did she know the details?

**Matthias:** *(looks down)* She went with him.

**Matthew:** I see.

**Matthias:** *(looks out)* She was the one who told them to go to Jerusalem in the first place. She said they should stop wandering around and get directions.

**Matthew:** I wondered about that.

**Matthias:** *(leans forward and looks at Matthew)* But, you know, it made perfect sense. Besides the asking for directions, I mean. *(stands and begins pacing)* Jerusalem was the capitol city of Judea, and my father and those he traveled with were very important men. It was only right that they visit the monarch of the land and announce their presence to him. Otherwise, they might have been perceived as spies or troublemakers. *(pauses)* Of course, they had no idea that their presence would cause such great disturbance for Herod and the people of Jerusalem. *(looks out and speaks quietly)* If my mother had known what would happen ...

**Matthew:** *(interrupts)* There was no way she could have known.

**Matthias:** She was haunted by it every day for the rest of her life. I'm sure that's why she persuaded my father to return to Jerusalem.

**Matthew:** Yes. We'll get back to that. *(looks at paper)* I would like to hear a little more about the first trip *(looks at Matthias)*, especially now that I know the source is truly reliable.

**Matthias:** *(sits rapidly and leans forward)* Right. Well, as my mother tells it, she and my father joined the caravan a little late. You see, my father always had trouble getting out of the tents on time ...

*(Lights dim stage right and come up stage left. Wise Man 1 is seated and examining the duffel bags and Wise Man 2 is seated and warming his hands at an imaginary fire. Wise Man 3 should stand as lights come up and be staring at Wise Man 4.)*

**Wise Man 1:** *(looks up)* Is it still there?

**Wise Man 4:** Yep.

**Wise Man 3:** Can you see it clearly?

**Wise Man 4:** Yep.

**Wise Man 2:** *(looks at Wise Man 4)* Is it still in the same place?

**Wise Man 4:** Yep.

**Wise Man 1:** *(stands)* You're sure it hasn't moved?

**Wise Man 4:** Yep.

**Wise Man 3:** *(leans over toward Wise Man 2)* Pssst. Hey, where'd we pick this guy up?

**Wise Man 2:** *(stands)* I don't remember. He and his wife just kind of appeared one day in the caravan.

*(Wise Man 1 walks over to Wise Man 2 and Wise Man 3, Wise Man 4 moves in front of stage block.)*

**Wise Man 3:** Do we know where they're from?

**Wise Man 2:** Not sure. Where does it look like they're from?

**Wise Man 3:** Now how am I supposed to tell that?

**Wise Man 2:** I don't know. Sometimes you can tell just by looking.

**Wise Man 1:** Yeah, and sometimes you get yourself into a lot of trouble that way.

**Wise Man 3:** Do you know where he came from?

**Wise Man 1:** Not me. I can't seem to get anything but one-word answers out of him.

**Wise Man 2:** Have you tried asking him where he's from?

**Wise Man 1:** I assumed he wanted to stay anonymous. *(gestures toward Wise Man 4)* He didn't bring any entourage with him — no one except his wife, that is — he didn't announce his arrival with any fanfare, and all he's done since he joined us is keep looking at that star. *(points up)*

**Wise Man 2:** Well, I'm going to ask. *(walks over to Wise Man 4)*

**Wise Man 1:** Good luck.

*(Wise Man 1 and Wise Man 3 move slightly to stage left.)*

**Wise Man 2:** Hey, there.

**Wise Man 4:** Yep.

**Wise Man 2:** *(motions toward star)* Pretty bright, isn't it?

**Wise Man 4:** Yep.

**Wise Man 2:** So, we *(gestures toward Wise Man 1 and Wise Man 3)* noticed that you and your wife joined us a few days back.

**Wise Man 4:** Yep.

**Wise Man 2:** Where, uh, where do you ... I mean ... that is to say, there do you two call home?

**Wise Man 4:** Back there.

**Wise Man 2:** *(nods head)* Back there. Anywhere in particular "back there"?

**Wise Man 4:** Nope.

**Wise Man 2:** Ah. *(stares at Wise Man 4 for a moment, then rejoins Wise Man 1 and Wise Man 3)*

**Wise Man 1:** See what I mean?

**Wise Man 2:** Slightly non-communicative.

**Wise Man 1:** That's an understatement.

**Wise Man 3:** And why do you suppose he brought his wife along? This is not a short journey.

**Wise Man 2:** Maybe that's why.

**Wise Man 3:** I beg your pardon?

**Wise Man 2:** *(sits on block)* Maybe he brought her because he knew what a long and arduous journey this would be and he didn't want to be without her for that long.

**Wise Man 1:** Quite the romantic, aren't you?

**Wise Man 2:** I get it from my wife. I do miss her.

**Wise Man 3:** *(moves to duffel bag, pulls out small bag, and looks in it while talking)* So, why didn't you bring *your* wife along?

**Wise Man 2:** *(looks up with a dreamy look on his face)* I promised her when we wed that she would never spend a night without a solid roof to cover her head and a warm bed to shelter her sleep.

**Wise Man 1:** *(walks over and sits on other block)* Ah. She wouldn't come?

**Wise Man 2:** *(opens duffel bag and looks through it)* Right.

**Wise Man 1:** I had to promise my wife that I would bring back a special gift for her.

**Wise Man 2:** Mine desires a special gift and several mementos from Palestine. *(pauses, Wise Man 1 and Wise Man 3 look at him)* She's quite a collector.

**Wise Man 3:** *(stands and holds up small bag)* Well, speaking of gifts, smell this. *(walks to Wise Man 1 and Wise Man 2 and lets each sniff)* So, what do you guys think?

**Wise Man 1:** Very nice. Where'd you find it?

**Wise Man 3:** I had my servants comb the marketplace for the most fragrant frankincense they could find. My servants have good noses.

**Wise Man 1:** *(smells bag again)* Mmmmmm. I can tell.

**Wise Man 2:** *(pulls small jar out of his duffel bag)* Well, as long as we're sharing, feel this. *(lets Wise Man 1 and Wise Man 2 sample the contents)*

**Wise Man 3:** Very sticky. Nice. *(stands and snaps his fingers)* I've got it! I know where you're from!

**Wise Man 2:** *(sits)* What?

**Wise Man 3:** *(walks between Wise Man 1 and Wise Man 2)* Your gift just gave you away! Myrrh is made from vegetation found in India, Arabia, and eastern Africa. So you're Indian, Arabian, or African!

**Wise Man 2:** Brilliant deduction. You sound like a walking encyclopedia.

**Wise Man 3:** Why, thank you.

**Wise Man 1:** I didn't realize you were that intent on discovering our nationalities.

**Wise Man 3:** I just thought it would be nice for posterity to know.

**Wise Man 2:** Do you really think people will care?

**Wise Man 3:** Some will, I'm sure.

**Wise Man 2:** Why?

**Wise Man 3:** Why am I sure?

**Wise Man 2:** No, why do you think they'll care?

**Wise Man 3:** Oh, well, that's easy. It's human nature.

**Wise Man 1:** It's human nature to care?

**Wise Man 3:** No, no, no. *(walks to stage right around Wise Man 1)* I mean it's human nature to be curious and to be interested in the details, such as who we are and what our origins are. *(turns toward Wise Man 4)* Now, if only I could figure out where that guy came from ...

**Wise Man 1:** *(interrupts)* Well, how about me? Do you know what land I call home?

**Wise Man 3:** What's your gift?

**Wise Man 1:** Actually, I went in with him on the myrrh.

**Wise Man 3:** Hmmmm. That confuses things a bit, doesn't it?

**Wise Man 2:** What about the new guy? Does anyone know what he's giving?

**Wise Man 1:** *(gestures toward box)* I believe that box filled with gold would be his.

**Wise Man 3:** Gold? *(throws hands up in exasperation)* Well, that doesn't help me at all!

**Wise Man 2:** You could always ask him. Perhaps you might succeed where I have failed.

**Wise Man 3:** You think?

**Wise Man 2:** I say it's worth a try. *(pauses)* For posterity and all.

**Wise Man 3:** *(nods head and looks determined)* Right. For posterity.

**Wise Man 2:** For posterity!

**Wise Man 3:** *(walks over to Wise Man 4)* Uh — greetings!

**Wise Man 4:** Yep.

**Wise Man 3:** *(looks up toward the star)* So, I see that you're still keeping close watch on the star.

**Wise Man 4:** Yep.

**Wise Man 3:** Good. That's good. That's a good thing.

**Wise Man 4:** Yep.

**Wise Man 3:** Yes, that's good because if it had moved at all, we would certainly want to know about it.

**Wise Man 4:** Yep.

**Wise Man 3:** Right. Well. So, um, we were just showing each other the gifts that we've brought to give the new king when we find him.

**Wise Man 4:** Yep.

*(Wise Man 1 and Wise Man 2 stand and move upstage right as Wise Man 3 begins speaking.)*

**Wise Man 3:** Yes, and well, you see, I had been able to deduce, that is, I had determined that the myrrh came from, well, so if the myrrh came from there, then it would logically stand to reason that perhaps the individual carrying the myrrh would also ... *(from here, continues mouthing words and gesturing as if he is still speaking)*

**Wise Man 1:** He's dying over there.

**Wise Man 2:** Should we rescue him?

**Wise Man 1:** I don't know. I'm kind of enjoying this.

**Wise Man 3:** *(begins speaking out loud again)* ... so the point is, I am at an absolute loss to tell where you are from since the gift you bear could come from just about anywhere.

**Wise Man 2:** That was poetic.

**Wise Man 1:** Very.

**Wise Man 3:** Do you understand my dilemma?

**Wise Man 4:** Yep.

**Wise Man 3:** Very good. So then you'll help me out by telling me where you're from?

**Wise Man 4:** Speak to the wife.

**Wise Man 3:** Well, now, there's a very ... *(looks at Wise Man 4)* I'm sorry, did you just speak more than two words in a row?

**Wise Man 4:** Yep.

**Wise Man 3:** Could you possibly repeat what you just said?

**Wise Man 4:** Nope.

**Wise Man 3:** No. I don't suppose you would. Well, speak to your wife. That sounds like an excellent idea.

*(All Wise Men freeze; lights dim stage left and come up stage right where Matthew is seen writing. As the scene begins with Matthew and Matthias, all Wise Men move everything off to stage left. Wise Man 2, Wise Man 3, and Wise Man 4 get their gifts and move into position for the next scene. Wise Man 4 is farthest stage right, Wise Man 1 next to him, then Wise Man 2, then Wise Man 3, all in a loose semicircle, facing out toward audience.)*

**Matthias:** And that's when my mother told them to head for Jerusalem.

**Matthew:** *(still writing, doesn't look up)* Did she ever tell them where you were from originally?

**Matthias:** I don't believe she did, no.

**Matthew:** *(looks at Matthias)* I don't suppose you would be interested in sharing that information?

**Matthias:** You know, I would, but I just don't think it's all that pertinent to the story.

**Matthew:** Maybe not.

**Matthias:** Suffice it to say that they all traveled from the East toward Judea.

**Matthew:** *(writes again)* Got it. *(looks up at Matthias)* So, they arrived in Jerusalem, spoke to Herod, and he sent them on their way to Bethlehem.

**Matthias:** The only reason he did that is because they told him where the king would be born. They were most definitely not of the sons of Israel, and yet they knew your prophecies better than your own king.

**Matthew:** That's not so hard to believe of Herod the "Legend-in-his-own mind" Great.

**Matthias:** He certainly did enough to make his name remembered.

**Matthew:** And loathed. So, was your mother able to recount the details of what happened when they finally found the child?

**Matthias:** You might be surprised by this, but my mother actually went along with them.

**Matthew:** Somehow, that doesn't surprise me at all.

**Matthias:** But, of course, she kept herself well hidden, so only my father knew she was there ...

*(Matthew begins writing again. The lights dim stage right and come up stage left. All Wise Men are facing forward, slightly stage right, looking at their surroundings.)*

**Wise Man 2:** This is it.

**Wise Man 4:** Yep.

**Wise Man 3:** The star has definitely stopped here.

**Wise Man 4:** Yep.

**Wise Man 1:** This doesn't look like a palace.

**Wise Man 4:** Nope.

**Wise Man 2:** Certainly not what I expected.

**Wise Man 1:** I was thinking something a little less — thatchy.

**Wise Man 3:** But the star has stopped here. This must be the place.

**Wise Man 1:** *(looks at Wise Man 2)* So, what do we do?

**Wise Man 2:** We could try knocking.

**Wise Man 1:** What if we're disturbing them?

**Wise Man 3:** Maybe someone should have thought of that earlier.

**Wise Man 2:** Don't you think they would be happy to see us? I mean, this is a rather — humble dwelling, and we do bring gifts of great worth.

**Wise Man 1:** But what if the family is trying to stay incognito? That must be it. Why else would they be here in this place?

**Wise Man 3:** Again, I repeat ...

**Wise Man 2:** *(interrupts and steps forward)* No. We came because we were led. The star was unmistakable and the heavens would not lead us astray.

**Wise Man 1:** *(steps beside Wise Man 2)* So what do we do?

**Wise Man 3:** *(joins Wise Man 1 and Wise Man 2)* Haven't we visited that question already?

**Wise Man 1:** No one answered it to my satisfaction. *(Wise Man 4 moves diagonally, downstage right)* Hey! Wait, what's he ...

**Wise Man 2:** *(interrupts)* He's talking to someone.

**Wise Man 3:** It's a woman.

**Wise Man 1:** *(looks, trying to see something)* Can you see her?

**Wise Man 3:** No, I can just tell by the voice.

*(Wise Man 4 looks back at the other three and motions them forward.)*

**Wise Man 2:** He's looking back at us. I think he's — yes, he's definitely motioning for us to follow him.

**Wise Man 1:** Well, this is it. This is what we came for.

**Wise Man 3:** Here we go.

*(All act as if they are entering a house.)*

**Wise Man 3:** Thank you for allowing us to ... *(stops as if speechless, falls to knees in worship)*

**Wise Man 2:** We are most ... *(stops, as if speechless, falls to knees in worship)*

**Wise Man 1:** We are in awe ... *(stops, as if speechless, falls to knees in worship)*

*("We Three Kings" is sung here. If desired, the lyrics may be changed to "We wise men....")*

**Wise Man 4:** Posterity will serve him; it will be told of the Lord to the coming generation. They will come and will declare his righteousness to a people who will be born, that he has performed it ... All the ends of the earth will remember and turn to the Lord, and all the families of the nations will worship before you (Psalm 22:30-31, 27 NASB).

*(Lights dim stage left and come up stage right. Matthias should stand just before the lights come up and face stage left as Wise Man 4 is finishing his line. During this scene all Wise Men replace the stage blocks and props as in their first scene.)*

**Matthew:** Wait a minute, wait a minute. Your father? Your father, who doesn't seem able to speak in complete sentences, quoted a song of David?

**Matthias:** *(turns to Matthew)* My mother swears to it. I guess there's an awful lot about my father that never really made sense. But one thing I can tell you is that although he almost never spoke much more than a single word at a time, when he did manage to make a coherent statement, it was usually pretty significant.

**Matthew:** Well, if he came out with things like that very often, I'd say you were the master of understatement. So did he know what he was saying? I mean, did he understand what the words meant — who David was talking about?

**Matthias:** It's difficult to say what my father understood. You know, the whole "not-speaking-in-complete-sentences" thing.

**Matthew:** That would make it difficult, yes.

**Matthias:** *(sits)* Whether he understood what he was saying or not, my mother claims that my father was a changed man after they returned home from Jerusalem.

**Matthew:** Changed in what way?

**Matthias:** Well, it's not as if he became an eloquent public speaker or anything like that. She said that he seemed more alive, more passionate about things than he had ever been before.

**Matthew:** Passionate?

**Matthias:** Okay, understand that this is my father we're talking about ... more passionate for him meant saying, "Definitely" instead of just, "Yep."

**Matthew:** Right.

**Matthias:** But for him it was a change. And it was a big step — four syllables instead of one. It was a pretty big deal.

**Matthew:** So were the others as affected as your father?

**Matthias:** *(leans forward)* Now that's the funny thing. My mother said that they were all of the same mind while they were in the house and in the presence of the child and his mother. And all had the same dream about not returning to Herod, so they chose a different route home. But that's when trouble set in....

*(Lights dim stage right and come up stage left.)*

**Wise Man 2:** *(sitting and warming his hands by the fire, says sarcastically)* This was a superb idea.

**Wise Man 3:** Yes, well, I didn't hear any complaints from you when we left Judea.

**Wise Man 2:** *(looks at Wise Man 3)* That's because you said we should trust you. "I know the best route," you said. "We'll be home in no time and Herod will never be the wiser."

**Wise Man 1:** *(looks at gift for his wife)* I think we all would have been a little wiser not to listen to Mr. Posterity over there.

**Wise Man 3:** *(walks stage right)* Okay, so our pack animals bolted when the storm set in and we lost most of our supplies. But that storm could have happened anywhere, anytime, to any one of you.

**Wise Man 2:** It did happen to us.

**Wise Man 3:** I rest my case.

**Wise Man 1:** *(stands)* This is getting us nowhere. I say we split up and each try to find our own way back.

**Wise Man 3:** What about safety in numbers?

**Wise Man 1:** *(looks at Wise Man 3)* I think we'd all be safer if our numbers didn't include you.

**Wise Man 3:** *(walks to Wise Man 1 and confronts him)* Is that so? Well, that is just fine with me. I've had enough of your simpering about your wife *(gestures toward Wise Man 2)*, and I'm definitely not going to miss you and your attitude. *(looks at Wise Man 1)*

**Wise Man 1:** *My* attitude? What attitude?

**Wise Man 2:** You do seem a bit negative at times.

**Wise Man 4:** Yep.

**Wise Man 1:** *(looks at Wise Man 4)* What do you know? That's it. I will not stand here and be insulted any longer.

**Wise Man 4:** Go back.

**Wise Man 1:** *(turns to Wise Man 4)* What?

**Wise Man 4:** Go back.

**Wise Man 1:** Back where?

**Wise Man 4:** Back there.

**Wise Man 1:** Why on earth would I want to do that?

**Wise Man 4:** Be changed.

**Wise Man 1:** *(stares at Wise Man 4 for a moment, then shakes head)* I have no idea what you're talking about. Fend for yourselves, gentlemen, I am going to find my own way home. *(grabs bag and exits stage left)*

*(Lights dim slowly stage left as all split up and go their separate ways — Wise Man 1 walks down the aisle, Wise Man 2 and Wise Man 3 look at each other, then Wise Man 2 exits stage left, while Wise Man 3 exits upstage left. The lights come up stage right.)*

**Matthias:** So after all that they had shared, after all that they had experienced together, it ended with them all scattering in bitterness.

**Matthew:** *(looks out)* I did not come to bring peace, but a sword (Matthew 10:34).[1]

**Matthias:** What's that?

**Matthew:** *(shakes head)* I'm sorry. I was just remembering something that I heard him say once.

**Matthias:** That's a strange thing for a man to say whose birth was heralded by a message of peace and good will to men.

**Matthew:** Peace on earth among men of good will (Luke 2:14).[2]

**Matthias:** I beg your pardon?

**Matthew:** You're referring to the message the shepherds heard on the night of his birth, right?

**Matthias:** Yes.

**Matthew:** They said, "Glory to God in the highest, and peace on earth among men of good will" (Luke 2:14).[3]

**Matthias:** That's what they said?

**Matthew:** Absolutely. Angels are so often misquoted.

**Matthias:** Aren't they, though?

**Matthew:** And of course, you can understand why. I mean, if you saw one angelic being, to say nothing of a whole host of them, your attention would probably be focused on things other than what they were saying.

**Matthias:** Whose wouldn't?

**Matthew:** Well, in any case, at least your father seemed to get the message, even if it wasn't delivered by an angel.

**Matthias:** Not by an angel, but by the Son himself. Like I said, he was a changed man after he left Bethlehem.

**Matthew:** I'm afraid he was.

**Matthias:** I'm glad my father's story will finally be told.

**Matthew:** Can you believe I've been listening all this time and I never even asked about names? Your father's I have, but I'll need the others. *(prepares to write and looks at Matthias expectantly)*

**Matthias:** Do you really? Do you really need them?

**Matthew:** Don't you think...?

**Matthias:** *(interrupts)* What, that posterity should know?

**Matthew:** I — oh — wait a minute ... *(writes)* So, tell me what you think of this — "Now after Jesus was born in Bethlehem of Judea in the days of Herod the king, behold, wise men from the East arrived in Jerusalem ..." (Matthew 2:1).[4]

*(Lights fade to black.)*

The End

---

1. Richard Lattimore, *The New Testament* (New York: North Point Press, 1997).

2. *Ibid.*

3. *Ibid.*

4. *Ibid.*

# Contributors

**Jeanne Mueller** is the elementary education director of the Maryland Agricultural Education Foundation. Currently a member of Catonsville Presbyterian Church in Catonsville, Maryland, Mueller has been a Sunday school teacher and religious education director for several congregations. A former elementary teacher, Mueller is an educational consultant and frequently leads teacher training workshops.

**Judith Hale Wood**, the illustrator of *Come! See What God Has Done*, attended the Maryland Institute of Art in Baltimore, and used her artistic ability professionally as an illustrator for the oceanography department at Johns Hopkins University. She currently resides in Kennett Square, Pennsylvania.

**Arthur J. L. Meether** is a former US Army officer and Lutheran pastor who now resides in Fergus Falls, Minnesota. He is a graduate of the University of Maryland, Wartburg Theological Seminary, and the Aquinas Institute of Theology.

**Judy Gattis Smith** is the author of more than a dozen books, including *Teaching the Mystery of God to Children* (CSS), *Teaching to Wonder*, *Planting Spiritual Seeds*, and *Developing a Child's Spiritual Growth through the Senses* (Abingdon). She has also written three books for grandmothers, and she is a regular contributor to *Episcopal Teacher* magazine. Smith has led more than 200 workshops and seminars, and has been a keynote speaker at conferences throughout the United States.

**Louis H. Valbracht** served as the pastor of Lutheran congregations in Ohio, Illinois, and Iowa, as well as a chaplain in the US Marine Corps. The author of ten books, Valbracht capped his lengthy career as the senior pastor of one of the largest Lutheran churches in America, St. John's Lutheran Church in Des Moines, Iowa.

**Janet Burton** is a pastor's wife, minister of education, and writer of Christian worship and education resources. She and her husband Jack, who have served churches in Texas and New Mexico for almost fifty years, reside in Austin, Texas, where Jack serves as an interim pastor for churches in transition. She is the author of five books (including a three-volume series of *Worship Innovations* for CSS) and a contributor to five others.

**Bill Thomas** is the pastor of Stony Point Christian Church in Kansas City, Kansas. An avid sports fan who is a football and basketball referee, he is the author of two young adult Christian books with a sports theme: *Pete Thompson and the Long Road Home,* and *Pete Thompson and the Last Out* (Publish America, 2004). He is also the author of *The Road to Victory* (CSS, 2007). Thomas is a graduate of the University of Kansas (B.S. in Education), Manhattan Christian College (B.Th.), and Johnson Bible College (M.A.).

**Robert V. Dodd** served for 31 years as a pastor of United Methodist congregations in western North Carolina. He is the author of eleven books and booklets, as well as a variety of curriculum resources. For a decade Dodd wrote the "Sunday School Lesson," a commentary on the weekly lessons in the International Series, for the *North Carolina Christian Advocate*. Dodd is a graduate of High Point University and Duke Divinity School.

**Myra Shofner** is a schoolteacher and freelance writer from Pensacola, Florida. Her writing credits include youth Sunday school curriculum for the SBC Sunday School Board (now Lifeway), numerous short stories and magazine articles, several novels, and a variety of plays for Contemporary Drama Service (Merriwether Publishing). She is also the author of two volumes of *The Ark Book of Riddles* (David C. Cook). An active member of Beulah Baptist Church in Pensacola, Shofner is a graduate of Mississippi College (B.S. in education) and the University of West Florida (M.A. in English literature).

**Donna J. Fetzer** is a professional storyteller from Wooster, Ohio, who has appeared in many states as well as on television and radio. She teaches classes in storytelling and playacting at several educational institutions, and often presents workshops at storytelling conferences. Fetzer originated "Grandma's Theater," and for the past fifteen years she has written, directed, and produced children's plays for her community. She is a member of St. Paul Lutheran Church in Smithville, Ohio.

**Adalya Hadar** (Rebekah McGhee) directs contemporary worship along with her husband, Gannon McGhee, at Pantano Baptist Church in Tucson, Arizona. She previously served as director of worship and arts at Northminster Presbyterian Church and Congregation Beth Sar Shalom (a messianic Jewish congregation) in Tucson. In each of these positions she has written and directed original theatrical productions as well as contemporary worship services. McGhee is also a member of Adalya, a band that has recorded two CDs (www.hadarpublications.com). She is a graduate of Grand Canyon University, with a B.A. degree in Christian Studies/Theatre.

www.ingramcontent.com/pod-product-compliance
Lightning Source LLC
Chambersburg PA
CBHW081217230426

43666CB00015B/2765